WINNING

AT

INTERVIEW

A New Way To Succeed

Alan Jones

3rd Edition

WINNING AT INTERVIEW

A New Way To Succeed (2017 Edition)

Copyright Alan Jones 2013

This edition 2017

All rights reserved

First published in paperback by Random House Business Books 2000

Cover design: www.creative-bytes.co.uk

Cover image: © iStockphoto/Palto

Other books by Alan Jones: 'How To Negotiate Your Salary' and 'Network To Get Work'

No part of this book may be reproduced, or transmitted in any form, or by any means, electronic or mechanical, including photocopying, recording, or by any information storage and retrieval system, without permission in writing from the author.

CONTENTS

Preface

Introduction

Chapter One
Getting In The Zone

Building Block 1 - What *Is* A Job?	13
Building Block 2 - What *Is* An Interview?	21
Building Block 3 - Keep Your Eyes On The Prize	26
Building Block 4 - Be Yourself?	31
Building Block 5 - The Two Guiding Principles	35
Building Block 6 - Selling Yourself The Best	38
Building Block 7 - You're Already A Winner	41
Building Block 8 - Helping Inexperienced Buyers	45

Chapter Two
The Removal Of Uncertainty

So - Communicate!	59
Having The Conversations With Yourself	65
Dead Zone One	70

Chapter Three
42 Questions - The Answer To Everything

So - Why Should I Hire You?	75
Weaving The Tapestry - The Subliminal Sell	119
Who's Got The Cheese? - A Cautionary Tale	144
A Word About Humility	160
Don't Shoot The Messenger	182
The End Game	202
Questions For You To Ask	210
Dead Zone Two And The 'Columbo Question'	226
Who's Got The Ball?	229

Extending The Olive Branch	234
Conclusion	237
Index of Questions	240

Preface

Why '*Winning* At Interview'? Well, as a job hunter you are clearly in a strong position if you are not competing with anyone. Yet, in reality there will be many occasions when you will be up against stiff competition. 'Winning At Interview' is a fitting title, as it reflects that competitive element, and to be the winner you must raise the bar on your performance to the highest of levels within your capability. This book will help you achieve that.

'A New Way To Succeed'? Random House first published this book in 2000 and in this 3rd edition (2017) I give much fresh insight, but still 'new' in that I advocate a different and unique approach to the subject of 'being interviewed for a job'. If you adopt and apply the principles I promote they will serve you well, as they have many thousands of people who have read it or attended my seminars over the years. Indeed, you may well have competed with them in the past - and lost.

So - If you're competing with others in a tough market be in no doubt you have a battle on your hands. You can't win today's battles with yesterday's weapons and just occasionally something new comes along which raises the bar and gives you the edge. 'Winning At Interview' is a paradigm shift as it takes a fresh look at how to prevail at interviews and win that job offer even when competing against others who may be better qualified and have more experience than you. Guard it jealously and do not let it fall into the hands of your competitors.

My thanks to all those thousands of 'sellers' and 'buyers' whose experiences have, over the past 30 years, given me the opportunity to produce this book for those who come after them.

---------♦ ♦ ♦---------

Introduction

All interviewers have been trained to interview. They have carefully studied your CV, fully understand the role they are seeking to fill, have carefully thought about the questions they need to ask you and have taken care to frame those questions in the right way. They also know what information and evidence they need from you in response to those questions. Or so you would think on reading other books about 'interview techniques'. In an ideal world this would be so, but my own experience throughout thirty years of working closely with job seekers and recruiters, *of all nationalities, across all disciplines and levels of seniority*, paints a very different picture. The reality is that only 2 out of 10 interviewers have been trained to interview. Yes, 80% of the people you're going to meet have no more experience of interviewing than you have of being interviewed. We must of course be careful about the conclusions we draw from such a statistic; those 8 out of 10 may still be astute, insightful and well prepared, just as the 2 out of 10 may have become jaded and lazy, but don't have a high expectation of what you may encounter out there. Now, this is a double - edged sword, for these inexperienced, untrained interviewers can, if you let them, cause you real problems, but if you are prepared they can present you with real opportunities. Why? Because your competitors will be facing those same people and if they are prepared at all they'll most likely only be prepared for the 2 out of 10, *and they are not the problem*. Should you be fortunate enough to be in front of a trained, experienced interviewer then you are in safe hands. Yes, they'll ask some tricky questions but will also give you plenty of opportunities to sell yourself. But they are as rare as hen's teeth. So, where is the value in preparing ourselves for the 'world of recruitment' as we would all like it to be? 'Winning At Interview' prepares you for the world of recruitment as it really is - an uncertain, unscientific world, a dark mysterious market place inhabited by sellers with little idea of what they are selling or how to sell it, and buyers unsure of their needs and how to fulfil them.

In 'Winning At Interview' I will not attempt to present you with what we might call 'a typical interview' where cause and effect are prescribed and outcomes predictable. There's no such thing as a 'typical interview' - for no two are the same. Each interview is a unique performance with its own dynamics, backdrop, entrances, exits and the important bit between the two. It is perhaps above all an exercise in communication in a competitive market. Winning the prize demands that *you communicate your truth in the most persuasive manner with which you are comfortable*. But, as I will reveal, what you say, how you say it or whether you choose to say it at all will change from interview to interview.

'Winning At Interview' is a book for the 21st century. It will show you how to head the hazards off at the pass by exposing myths, building your confidence, changing your perception of the interview process and encouraging you to break some traditional, and tired, old rules. In this game of 'Interview' you've more cards to play than you could ever have imagined – they have served my job-hunting friends well over the years. Read on and discover how to raise *your* game.

Chapter One

Getting in 'The Zone'

Two things determine the outcome of your performance at job interviews:

1. Your mind-set

2. Your preparation

Just one of the above is no good without the other. We'll work on the preparation in Chapters Two and Three but it is imperative we begin by ensuring you are in the right 'mind-set'.

Athletes often remark that doing the training is all very well but it won't pay dividends if, on the day of the race and when that gun goes off, they are not 'in the zone'. Interviews are exactly the same. You can prepare as much as you like but if you show up on the day and you're not 'in the zone' then that preparation is unlikely to pay off. *A confident and positive mental attitude is the single most defining feature that separates the winners from the losers* and in a competitive market confidence is King.

Interviews can be sprints or marathons but all are performances so you must be 'psyched up' before that gun goes off. To achieve this I will firstly reveal the 8 'building blocks' that get you 'in the zone'. Once in place they will be the platform on which we will build your preparation. Each one will independently serve you well but combined they are a powerful force.

Building Block 1 - What *Is* A Job?

Successful job hunting demands a complete change of mind-set. Time and again people say "I'm going to a job interview" but have no clear understanding of what a 'job' or 'interview' really is.

So, if you are going to a 'job interview' let us define terms. On a blank piece of paper draw a line across the middle, and above the line write down your answer to the question **'What *is* a Job?'**

Your answer may be a simple sentence or perhaps a list of words. There's no deep analysis required here – go with your instinctive response.

NOTE: This is the only 'exercise' you have to do – the rest is just an easy read. But it's important so please don't skip it.

Does your answer include any of these?

'It's what I do for a living'

'It's a way of filling my time'

'It's a means to an end'

'It's something I enjoy'

'It's a way of earning a salary'

'It gives me security'

'It gives me status'

'It allows me to learn and develop'

'It gives me routine and structure to my week'

'It's something that allows me to interact socially with people'

'It's a stepping stone on my career path'

If so *you are not in the zone* because it's all about you, is it not? The above (and it's worth noting that they are all the things you lose when redundancy strikes) may be what a job is *to you* but that wasn't the question and, as we'll see in Chapter Three, *understanding the question* is often the key that unlocks the door to success.

Now have another go at the question but this time abandon the 'job-seeking' mind-set, cast it to one side and instead enter the 'recruiter zone'. So, in effect, you're now the 'interviewer' and the person who has this 'job' to award. Below the line, write *your* answer to the same question **'What *is* a job?'**

If your answer comes close to *'a job is a means of fulfilling a need profitably'* (or 'cost effectively' if you are targeting the 'not for profit' sector) then Building Block 1 is just about in place. But let's add a little cement.

We now have two very different answers to the same question, and this will be useful in Chapter Three as it demonstrates that the same question can mean something entirely different depending on who is asking and who is on the receiving end. But it surely begs another question: "So what – how does this get me in the zone?" Well, it clarifies the true nature of the relationship between 'interviewee' and 'interviewer'. It's a 'seller'/'buyer' relationship. You have something to sell that the buyers need and they are willing to pay cash for it. *It's a business transaction.* No more, no less. There was a time when we liked to believe it was a bit cosier than that, but that was in the days when we thought these organisations* existed solely for the purpose of employing people. That no one *wants* to hire us is initially somewhat worrying, but it's nothing personal – they don't want to hire anyone else either. So, we must remove the emotional dynamic from the 'employer'/'employee' relationship and see it purely as the *business transaction* that it is. If you are presently in paid employment it is delusional to believe you are there for any other reason than to satisfy *their* 'below the line' need.

And yet, as sellers in a competitive market place we're often psychologically on the back foot because the buyer also has something *we* need, that 'job', and boy do we need it bad, and the greater our need the worse our performance.

Problems arise then because each party is working to a different agenda. The employer is seeking to find someone to fill a particular role, which is not always clearly defined, and the prospective employee is seeking to find a job. This dichotomy, where each party is dancing to a different tune, has proven to be the rock on which many an interview has foundered. This won't do. We must raise our game and we don't achieve that by becoming 'job beggars' – that's a recipe for a long stressful job search.

An interview is an exercise in communication and to win the prize you must send all the right signals to the buyer. Buyers don't respect job beggars because they send the signal loud and clear that *they* have the problem. Some even send the signal that they *are* the problem. The term 'job beggar' may seem unsympathetic and pejorative but I don't intend it to be – it's simply the way we are. This looms most large when we 'lose our job' because we lose all the 'above the line ' things that went with it. We then *take ownership of the problem* and become so emotionally engaged in solving our problem that this expresses itself in the signals we send: 'I've been made redundant and am writing to ask if you have any vacancies….' can be interpreted as 'I've got a problem and hope you can solve it by giving me a job'. Buyers don't care about the needs of sellers. No one cares what you are 'looking for'; no one cares that you are 'seeking a challenging opportunity'. Your personal 'objective' is of little or no interest to buyers. And because no one cares no one replies to job begging approaches. Because no one replies you don't get any feedback. No feedback means that you carry on making the same mistakes and your job search is a barren wasteland of disappointments and missed opportunities. If you're 'in the zone' you should get multiple interviews and multiple offers, even in a tough buyers' market.

There are then two types of 'interviewee'. The majority who, by virtue of what they say, how they say it and their body language clearly give the impression that the only reason they've turned up is to solve their problem and get a job – they are emotionally engaged in their 'above the line' needs. How could we blame a busy buyer for thinking "Hey, I'm not in business to solve your problem - I'm in business to make a profit - tell me how you can help me achieve that?". To win the prize and get the offer you must send this signal to the buyer:

' It's your lucky day. I'm giving you the chance to hire me because based on my understanding of your problem I'm the solution.' In cold print that may appear arrogant but those people get respect and they get hired. The empowering thing is this: *you can decide which one you want to be.* If it were only possible for me to give you one interview tip it would be this: *During the interview the more interest you show in their problem the more likely it becomes, far more likely, that you're the one who's asked to solve it.* Be 'in the zone' by drilling down on their 'below the line' needs and you will secure your 'above the line' needs. In other words become 'customer focussed' - a term you perhaps haven't come across before.

This building block should underpin your whole approach not solely to interviews but to your whole job search campaign. For example, don't react to a job advertisement by thinking 'that could be a job for me', or in other words 'that could solve my problem'. An 'in the zone' reaction is: 'That's a problem crying out for a solution and that could be me'. 'A problem crying out for a solution' is a pretty neat definition of a job advertisement.

'To get a job you have to forget that you are looking for one' is a neat paradox that will serve you well.

You are no longer 'looking for a job', for that is a job-begging phrase. You are looking for a problem to solve and they have it. It's worth repeating - *successful job hunting demands a complete change of mind-set*. Take any other view and here's what will happen - your CV will disappear into that mysterious black hole - that repository for all the shattered hopes and dreams of your competitors. It will reside alongside theirs and there it will remain, unread and unloved. Resistance to Building Block 1 is futile.

* I will use the more neutral and inclusive 'organisations' throughout the book as you may be selling into the public/not for profit sectors.

Building Block 2 - What *Is* An Interview?

Now we know what a job is we can tackle that word 'Interview'. Roll it around your tongue for a while. How does it taste? If it were not so serious we might burst out laughing. It's quite astonishing that we continue to do these things to each other in the 21st century. 'An interview is a two-way process' has become a cliché, but why so? Because the word 'interview' doesn't readily convey that it's two-way that's why – and far from it; it conveys that it's all one-way – the interviewers' way. The very word 'interview' can make you nervous and put you on the back foot. It is so damaging and yes, so risible, we won't use it for much longer.

The changing world of work in the late 19th and early 20th century spawned an almost patrician language to describe the ways in which labour was bought and sold; 'job,' 'employee,' 'retirement,' 'salary', 'indenture' and yes, 'interview' were used before then but were now more commonplace. We became stuck with them, but they *belong* to the 20th century and that's where we'll leave them, as they won't serve us well in the 21st. To ease this transition our language, and our mind-set, must shift accordingly. That damaging, morale sapping emotional baggage pervading the job-begging culture must be jettisoned if we're to adapt to this new world of work and this book will reflect that. The 'job' is something we'll leave behind – it's no longer a neat way to parcel up work. Welcome to the gig economy!

But while we're at it let's be bold and consign the word 'interview' to the historical garbage can. It's no longer fit for purpose. It's not a grown up, mature word for the 21st Century and I for one won't mourn its passing – it was always too close to 'interrogation' and 'inquisition' (those three words are bedfellows and unsettling). For sure, you will still find yourself attending 'interviews' for 'jobs' in the old fashioned sense for some time yet as not everyone has caught on, but having removed all the emotion and understood that this is no more than a business transaction it makes more sense to see these 'interviews' for what they really are; they are *business meetings* where you, the seller, are seeking to persuade the buyer to hire your services. As we've seen in BUILDING BLOCK 1 the buyer is the one with the problem – *you're the solution*. Keep that as a slogan on your screen saver – it'll buoy you up no end every day. Who knows, if all 'sellers' stopped using the word 'interview' the buyers might stop using it too – and what a step into the 21st Century that would be.

BUILDING BLOCK 2 is a guiding principle to which you must adhere at all times. It underpins your approach to, and your conduct during, the meeting. From now on you'll conduct yourself as you would conduct yourself at any other business meeting. The feedback I get on this is remarkable - you will find that reframing it in your own mind as a 'meeting' will empower and liberate you, not least because it more readily conveys that it's a two-way process. Self-employed people don't go to 'interviews' so why should you?

To illustrate this let's take an example: So many sellers, and mature, experienced people at that, have asked me, and the way they phrase the question is telling, "Are you allowed (*allowed*?) to make notes during the interview?" My response is: 'Would you be asking me that question if you were going to any other business meeting?' "No, I'd either make notes or I wouldn't". 'Then why are you asking me now?' Let's not leave that swinging in the breeze – no two meetings are the same, each one is a unique event with its own 'dynamics' and 'undertows'. What you do, what you say, how you say it or whether you say it at all will change, sometimes in subtle ways, from meeting to meeting and you'll be exercising your judgment across a whole range of issues. This is just one of them. But it's either a two-way process or it isn't. It can't be two-way in some respects but not in others. So, we're either in or we're out and if the buyers are taking notes, and not even entertaining the question 'am I allowed?' then why sellers choose to put themselves psychologically on the back foot in this way is a mystery. By the way, if you choose to make notes be selective and don't take dictation as it can un-nerve the buyer and you lose that all important eye contact that you wouldn't want to lose at any business meeting. So when the buyer says 'good morning' don't write it down.

It is necessary to add a caveat to the above, for there are subtleties about the process that I will endeavour to get across as the chapters unfold. Be mindful - what zone are *they* in when you turn up? Their mind-set may be quite different to yours and if they are determined to give you a good old-fashioned 'interview' then you have to give a little. For example, when you announce yourself at reception by saying "I have a 2pm *meeting* with Sarah Smith", and they look up at you and reply, as they assuredly will, "Ah, you've come for the *interview*", I don't suggest that you reach over, lift them up by the lapels and re-educate them; that's called 'winning the battle but losing the war'. So do tread softly - but across the course of a meeting you can gently coax them into understanding that this is more of a two-way process than they believed it to be. After twenty minutes you may just see the scales lifting from their eyes.

Building Block 3 - Keep Your Eyes On The Prize

Have clarity on your objective and stick to it. Your primary objective in turning up for the meeting is to ultimately get the buyer to make you an offer, which you don't have until you've got it in writing. *Until you have accepted that written offer the deal isn't done and you have no decision to make.* If I could put that sentence in neon lights I would, for in losing sight of your objective you can lose more than you might ever know.

Sellers have an alarming habit of making a pre-emptive decision *during the meeting* that they don't want to solve the buyers' problems. This is a common mistake and all too easy to understand why it happens. We could accurately describe the meeting as a 'fact-finding tour' for both parties. The tour may take in two, three or more meetings. Play it long and see the process as a gradual 'harvesting' of facts. You won't have all the facts, on which to base a sound judgment, until you receive the written offer. Even then there may be issues that require further clarification. Problems arise when buyers divulge 'facts' about their problem, their business, their perceived solution and not least the price, which serve to make you feel less than enamoured of the whole shebang.

If you've forgotten BUILDING BLOCK 1 and are focused on *your* needs then your attitude and demeanour will reflect this through visible lack of enthusiasm and a diminishing performance. This can be infectious. If the buyer catches it you will reach a mutual decision that there's no point in taking it to the next stage. That's a round one knockout to the buyer. Now ok, if you're uncovering so many negative facts that it's clear this is a complete mismatch then you may as well throw your cards on the table and say so - but don't let one or two negative facts switch you off. Here's why:

Firstly, *don't assume that buyers know what they're looking for or even understand the extent of their problem.* This is especially true of an exploratory networking meeting, where very little may be defined and where you may be talking to a 'gatekeeper' and not the person who has the problem (that's the one you want to get in front of at the next meeting). First meetings in particular are fertile ground for misunderstanding and miscommunication. I've worked with many sellers who, having received a good offer, are grateful to have stayed true to their objective; issues that appeared insurmountable during the stress and strain of the first meeting had either paled into insignificance or disappeared altogether by the time the offer was made.

Also remember that everything, not least the price, is more negotiable at the offer stage than at any time leading up to it. The turbulent waters of these meetings can throw up a lot of garbage. Navigate your way through, put clear water between yourself and your competitors and then make an informed decision in the calmer waters of your own territory.

Across a three month recruitment process the buyer's need may be evolving in surprising ways - to such an extent that it may even disappear altogether - which is one reason you should never take your foot off the gas.

Secondly, It's not uncommon to find yourself subsequently being invited to solve a problem other than the one you've turned up to discuss. Here's how this one might work. Maybe two months ago you responded to an advertisement. Not the right thing for you really but hey, you didn't have anything else to do that day so thought you'd limber up and go for it. Today they invite you to go and meet them. You may be inclined to turn it down on the basis that you don't want the job – an extreme example of making a pre-emptive decision. But quite rightly you decide to show up because you understand that you need all the practice you can get and why turn down a networking opportunity?

Now, as buyers we can decide, perhaps within ten minutes, that sellers are not the right solution for this particular problem or that they are underselling themselves; but if they maintain their enthusiasm for the role and by inference (and this is the important 'undertow') their enthusiasm for working with us, then we'd most likely be considering them for something better, maybe something we hadn't got around to advertising. But if we see their enthusiasm visibly waning, and their performance dimming, why would we go there? It's worth emphasising that all meetings are gold dust, as it takes about 6 meetings to reach peak performance, so never turn down any opportunity to put yourself in front of a stranger and hone your selling skills.

Incidentally, the buyers may not take the 'better' role off the shelf and show it to you. They wouldn't want to raise your expectations nor send signals that they were not seriously considering you for the role you have come to discuss. It's also likely that this 'hidden' role is very embryonic in their mind and/or they may still have internal battles to fight to get approval for hiring.

So, remember that when you are on those starting blocks and that gun is about to go off, you must be 'in the zone' but you may have plenty of hurdles to jump - the prize is that finishing tape in the distance. Keep your eyes on that prize.

If you are selling yourself in a small, insular market place where buyers may know each other, you won't want to get a reputation for being a time-waster so exercise sound judgment and decide when it is time to withdraw gracefully from the discussions.

Building Block 4 - Be Yourself?

Beware the well-meaning advice to 'be yourself' – it's not worth a hill of beans. This doesn't mean you must try to be someone else or try to change your innate character and personality – far from it, they're big selling points - hopefully. It's just that the advice is too simplistic. As human beings we are not one-dimensional – we are multi-faceted and thus have different 'behaviours'.

When people advise 'be yourself' they are, without realising it, giving you permission to do no preparation – WYSIWYG (What You See Is What

You Get). They are in effect saying: 'You're a nice person, everyone thinks you're a nice person so go along and be a nice person and you'll be fine.' Now I've met a lot of nice people at these business meetings and it's been a real pleasure to be in their company; they have been personable, engaging and made me smile but they have also left me hugging an empty sack. They have left no credible evidence on the table that they can solve the problem other than that they are nice human beings.

We might not like it but there's some benign artificiality about these meetings and it requires a degree of gaming to get through them, for both buyer and seller. To a greater or lesser extent we all role-play in a business situation. For example, the signals we send to a colleague are different to those we might send to a customer or client and we learn to differentiate instinctively – different strokes for different folks. But because we're not frequently in a selling situation it's not instinctive for us to realise the need to do this. A professional boxer may well be a most affable person outside the ring but the coach would be ill advised to say 'just go in that ring and be yourself.' That contest would only last ten seconds.

In a professional situation we try to present the image the other party expects, and deserves, to see. It's no more than a professional courtesy. Problems arise when either seller, or buyer, or both, fail to understand the need to role-play. Both parties must have their 'business hat' on their heads and not their 'social hat'. Now many a seller has turned up with their 'business hat' on their head but left the meeting an hour later with their 'social hat' perched at a cocky angle, because either the buyer has been an unprofessional 'social hat' or has been so professional and subtle in their interviewing that the seller has let their guard down. Why is it that when these meetings take place in a social setting e.g. over lunch, they are notoriously tricky to handle? Because in those situations the informality of the occasion seduces us into being our 'social selves' and this is reflected in not necessarily what we say but *how* we say it.

As the seller you're very much in the hands of the buyer and as such you must be prepared to follow their lead and adapt to the prevailing degree of formality/informality. But turn up with your business hat firmly on your head and make sure you leave with that business hat still firmly in place.

Much has been written and said about so called 'interview techniques' and yes, there are techniques we can and should utilise, as do the buyers. And yet the word 'techniques' is unhelpful as it suggests an *unnecessary degree* of artificiality. I have always approached 'interview coaching' not as imparting 'techniques' but as a means of ensuring the delivery of a professional, quality service to the buyer, based on preparation, courtesy and sound common sense. We shall also see in BUILDING BLOCKS 5 & 8 that it's not just about selling yourself to get the offer but *helping the buyer to make the right decision*. You have to leave them with more than just a warm glow so do give yourself up completely to the idea that you are turning up to give a performance. If you do not embrace that idea then by default you have lowered the bar on your performance before the curtain goes up.

Building Block 5 - The Two Guiding Principles

Always stick to the guiding principles of truth and supportability (and if something is true it is always supportable). Yes, you may consider this to be a novel idea in a post truth era but there is no room for hype either on a CV or at these meetings. Getting yourself hired isn't about telling lies or exaggerating your capability. To do so is wrong, period. *It's about articulating your truth in the most persuasive manner with which you are comfortable.* And yet one of the interesting but sad 'dynamics' of these meetings is that 'nerves' and lack of preparation can cause us to dissemble and, as we shall see in BUILDING BLOCK 6, modesty can conceal the truth.

A person of my acquaintance was at a meeting to discuss an administrative role. Apparently all was well until he was faced with the question (page 110): "What's your greatest weakness?" He replied, in effect, "I'm not great at administration." Naturally enough this showstopper knocked him out of the game. Now this was a puzzle, as I knew him to be an excellent administrator, so why did he say otherwise? "Well, there were three of them sitting there and I felt outgunned. I hadn't prepared for the question, the silence was deafening and, though I realised how dangerous the question was, my brain seized up and I just said the first crazy thing that came into my head." Through lack of preparedness he admitted to a weakness he didn't have. He gave up on the question, lost the plot and was out of the game. Maybe it served him right for telling a lie?

Other people respond to the question (page 95): "Why did you leave your previous employer?" by saying "I was made redundant." Another lie – *jobs* are made redundant, not people.

We saw in BUILDING BLOCK 3 that buyers can in effect mess up, particularly at a first meeting, by communicating 'facts' that are at best misleading if not plain wrong. Well, it's a two-way process so of course sellers can do the exact same thing. For example, sellers will admit to a weakness they have which in reality gives no cause for alarm in the workplace but which, once revealed as 'a truth' at these meetings, will assume a significance in the mind of the buyer that it simply doesn't deserve. It can be like throwing a bone to a pack of starving hounds – it's pounced on, chewed over, spat out and pounced on again, with the bemused seller wondering why the heck the buyers are slavering over it so much. In such ways can 'the truth' become distorted and thus your enemy.

In no way are these meetings an exact science. Getting hired and hiring people is an art form and it's the shades of grey that can enthral, raise a smile or draw a tear.

Should you need any more convincing then consider this: Think about your colleagues in your present or previous place of work. Some of them I'm sure were really on top of their game and respected by all. Others were average, some mediocre and some downright bad (and which category are you in?). Well, if recruiting people was such an exact science how come all those poor performers got themselves hired?

Your CV must be robust and credible. Too often as a buyer I have met sellers who are victims of their own hyperbole. For example, a statement on a CV such as 'Excellent leadership skills' invites the question: "How can you demonstrate that your leadership skills are excellent as opposed to being just 'good'?" You don't want to be looking like a rabbit in the headlights. If that seller had already been presenting at least some of the attributes we might associate with an 'excellent' leader e.g. inspirational, then the question may not have been posed as they would have seen that excellent leader sitting in front of them. 'Excellent' is a strong word to use so use it sparingly and wisely. Who could forgive the buyer from thinking 'If I can't believe that then I can't believe anything'. Veer away from the path of truth and your CV tumbles like a pack of cards along with your credibility at the meeting.

It's not that you can't use superlatives but without the substance to back them up they are at best unhelpful.

Building Block 6 - Selling Yourself The Best

Time to expose perhaps the greatest myth of all. In the world of recruitment we like to believe that it's all about hiring the best available person. It isn't. Well, it is in the sense that as buyers that's what we strive to achieve. And yet the vagaries and 'grey areas' are such that invariably the best people don't even get to show up to the meeting. Why is this? Because they had sub-standard CV's, that's why. Or maybe they got to the first meeting (you can get invited to a meeting *despite* the quality of your CV not because of it - in a sellers' market buyers often have to pick the best of a bad bunch) but they got no further. Why? Well, maybe because they weren't the right person, perhaps because they didn't know the first five building blocks, but most likely because they didn't know this building block – *we always hire the ones who sold themselves the best* - always – either by luck or judgment. The two don't have to be mutually exclusive but on most occasions they are.

An awful lot of good people get rejected, not because they can't do the job, but because they haven't mastered the dark arts of persuading us that they can. And, exaggerating to make a point, a lot of awful people get hired because they have mastered those dark arts. That's the way it is.

Selling yourself (and, as we shall see, defending yourself) better than your competitors is the difference between winning and losing. To achieve this you have to overcome any natural modesty.

Modesty is an engaging trait to have when it's 'social hat' time but it won't serve you well at these meetings. If you're good at what you do then how will the buyer ever know unless you tell them? So here's the bottom line – in a competitive market you can't afford to be competing against other sellers who couldn't hold a candle to you professionally but who are quite prepared, and skilled enough, to sell whatever it is they have to sell. For they'll win and you'll lose - plain and simple.

This then is a nettle you have to grasp. Modesty is your enemy. To win you have to 'push the envelope' i.e. *take yourself out of your comfort zone and say things that won't come naturally to you.* But take comfort from Building Block 5.

Modesty is not helpful to the buyer, not least because, as we now know, most are not trained or skilled in the dark arts of buying. For that reason never assume they know what their problem is. Never assume they know why they're asking the questions they're asking and never assume they know what responses they're seeking from you. That way madness lies.

Building Block 7 - You're Already A Winner

Another person of my acquaintance told me of the time he was hiring and was swamped with over a hundred CV's. He said to his boss "How are we going to get through that lot?" His boss replied "That's easy" and threw half of the CV's, at random, into the trashcan. "Wha...that's not fair!" said my acquaintance. "Sure it's fair, we don't want to hire anyone who's that unlucky do we?" said the boss.

Assuming your CV gets through a more rigorous selection process than that take heart from this, and it will boost your confidence no end – you're already a winner! The fact-finding has already begun and they have decided to meet you because they like the facts they've read on your CV and perhaps in your powerful and persuasive cover letter. Others have been eliminated from the competition and, as we've seen, maybe the best person for the role was one of them.

So, you and your remaining competitors are all winners at the paperwork stage. But you are not all equal. There's a pecking order, often subliminal in the mind of the reader. Perhaps they've decided to meet you because, based on the facts they've read, you could *possibly* solve their problem. Your competitor may, on paper, have a higher credibility rating, where the buyer is saying ' Based on the facts I've read about you I believe you could *probably* be the solution to my problem.' But on arrival at the meeting this pecking order on paper can be turned on its head in less than ten seconds. The heart of many a buyer has sunk when a 'probable', who on paper appeared to be perfect, showed up with no spring in their step, a wet fish handshake, an unnerving problem with eye contact and the kind of face that only a mother could love. Yes, first impressions are dangerously subjective, but if it looks like a duck, walks like a duck and makes a noise like a duck – it's a duck! Protest if you must, but there was a reason Quasimodo worked in the bell tower and not on the gift counter.

Conversely, if the one with the weakest CV is brisk, businesslike, presentable, engaging and confident; if all the signals convey the message 'I really want to be here, tell me about your problem' then that person has already moved into the 'probable ' category before they have got their coat off. The buyers are onside immediately and now *want* that person to win the prize - they are fervently praying they don't screw up during the meeting. They are now likely to be more forgiving of perceived weaknesses on the CV. Another cliché for sure but you really don't get a second chance to make a first impression. Some lucky people can do this naturally but they are in the minority. The rest of us have to work hard at it. To win friends and influence people is really a matter of making the best of what the fates have given you, not least because first impressions are usually visual.

Logic dictates then that if you get the meeting it must surely be within your gift to win the prize and convert it to an offer. You wouldn't have been invited to the meeting if that weren't so. There are three provisos to this. You can win the offer if:

1. You turn up prepared and willing to *sell* what you have to offer.

2. You turn up prepared to *defend* yourself against objections the buyer may still have.

3. There's a level playing field.

As there's no point in worrying about those things you can't control then forget that final one above. On most occasions there is a level playing field i.e. all sellers at the meeting have a chance of winning the contest. If it's a done deal and they've already decided that, for example, an internal person will be promoted into the role, and they're just going through the motions of meeting external people to satisfy some equal opportunities legislation, then it wouldn't matter how well you, or your competitors, sold yourself or how well you defended yourself. But, as we'll see, on a level playing field selling and defending is the key to success. You may give a world-class first impression with a world-class CV, but you still have to sell during the meeting. Give an average first impression with an average CV then you have a sell harder than it could have been and perhaps more to defend. Give a bad first impression with any CV then you've lost before you've sat down. It's often said 'they make a decision on you in the first thirty seconds (2 minutes, 5 minutes - it depends on who's saying it)'. That's largely correct but to be clear, if a decision is made that early it's a decision *not* to hire, but when you walk into that meeting do so with the mind-set that you're already the winner and *it's yours to lose* - have that competitive spirit.

Building Block 8 - Helping Inexperienced Buyers

Buyers and sellers are not a different species. We all come from the same gene pool. And yet as sellers we're psychologically predisposed to believe otherwise. We believe the people we're going to meet have absolute clarity on their problem, have studied our CV, thoroughly prepared for the meeting, know what questions to ask, know why they're asking them and know what responses they want to hear. We also assume they've been trained to conduct these meetings in a professional manner. Make the mistake of assuming all that and you'll be on the back foot from the start. It's simply not so.

Most buyers may have read your CV, although most likely only glanced at it (experienced buyers will have *studied* it), but they will have had little or no training or experience, and most of them no more frequently recruit than you job hunt. They may even be more nervous than you are. Should you be fortunate enough to meet buyers who know what they're doing then you're in safe hands – they will give you great opportunities to sell yourself and, providing you're prepared, it's game on. When two 'social hats' (Building Block 4) are doing business it's amazing anyone gets hired. When buyers have their 'business hats' on and you're wearing your 'social hat' then someone may get hired but it won't be you.

If you apply the principles of 'Winning At Interview' then you will have your 'business hat' firmly fixed to your head at all times – but what if – and this is how it is much of the time - they are wearing their 'social hat'? Well, as some people don't know they need something until you start selling it to them you don't want to leave them hugging an empty sack when you've gone - you've just got to help them out and make sure you not only get your selling points across but leave them with the *evidence* to support what you're selling.

The remainder of this book will show you how to do this. 'Winning At Interview' doesn't focus on what used to be called 'types' of 'interview' e.g. 'structured', 'unstructured', 'formal', 'informal', 'competency based', panel, 1-1, 'Top Grading'. Why? Because there are really only two 'types' of meeting: well conducted meetings and badly conducted meetings. This book prepares you for the latter, the majority. If you can manage the bad ones then the good ones won't cause you a problem.

To convert meetings into offers you may then have to go beyond 'selling' and 'defending' against objections. It's also about *helping the buyer out*, making their job easy and giving them the *evidence* on which to base a sound judgment that you're worth hiring. As we shall see, this 'evidence' most often comes in the form of an *example* you may have to volunteer - and examples are the premise upon which 'competency based interviews' are founded. Examples back up what you are selling. Unfortunately only 2 out of 10 buyers will ask you for them.

If you know what to look for you can establish, in the first 5 minutes, whether you are sitting in front of the 2 out of 10 competent or 8 out of 10 not so competent buyers. *The sooner you can form this judgment the sooner you will know how much you may need to control and help them manage the meeting.* There is a subtlety to this; you don't wrest control of the meeting from the buyer. The art is for you to be in control but manage it in such a way that they believe they are in control.

What signs should you be looking for? Well, the really competent ones will have extended you the courtesy of investing time, even some of their own personal time, into their preparation, because they really understand how important this meeting is to you. As part of that preparation they would have *studied* your CV and any cover letter/email. You can be confident that they have a full understanding of their need, or the needs of their client if you are meeting with an agency. They will have thought carefully about what facts they need to get from you, and the *evidence* to support those facts; they will have carefully considered the questions they might need to ask of you - and how to frame those questions because, as we will see later, how a question is framed is critical; frame it badly and it's a 'rubbish in - rubbish out' conversation. Finally, they would have given some thought to the *environment* within which the meeting will take place. They don't always have a lot to work with but the good ones will put you at your ease, make the meeting seemingly informal and not be sitting behind a desk/table. As buyers we find that people give more of themselves in an informal setting than they ever would if you sat them behind a desk. All physical barriers should be removed. Those needing your help will have done few, if any, of these, but don't give them the evil eye as it's counter-productive - reach out and help them because it's not their fault. Incidentally, the overall standard of recruitment is far higher in the public/government and not for profit sectors than it is in the private sector - a generalisation but an observation worth making.

You now have all the building blocks in place. They are the solid foundation on which to build your preparation and ensure you show up to that meeting with the right attitude. They'll serve you well for what lies ahead.

---------♦ ♦ ♦-------

Chapter Two

The Removal of Uncertainty

The battle is won or lost before you even show up. It's really a matter of preparation and damage control. Imagine that in going to the meeting you're a ship sailing into a war zone. You'd be fortunate to sail away without having had a few holes blown in your rigging, but do your damage control before entering and you're equally unlikely to be sunk by the first salvo. It is perfectly natural, even advisable, to feel 'nervous' before the meeting. Most sellers are but for all the wrong reasons. Professional actors *expect* to feel nervous because they've attended all the rehearsals, they know their lines and when the curtain goes up they want all that hard work to be reflected in their performance. Amateurs (your competitors) will have missed a few rehearsals, be shaky on their lines, know it and be nervous when the curtain goes up because they're hoping that it won't show. It will. Let them be too busy being nervous to think about winning.

Be in no doubt – this is not a game of chance or luck (though we all need a bit of that) – no, it's a game of skill – skills and dark arts that you can learn to master. You are venturing into the unknown when going to these meetings and you don't want any surprises so preparing to win is about *the removal of uncertainty*. Remove that uncertainty and you'll be nervous for all the right reasons.

'Further to your application for the above position we have pleasure in inviting you to an interview at the above address at 2 p.m. on Friday 13 May. When you arrive please ask for Mr. John Smith.'

You're already a winner but any elation you may feel at having clinched the meeting should be tempered by a degree of curiosity. Your competitors may do no more than make a note in the diary and carry on snoozing. If you snooze, you lose. On receipt of an invitation to a meeting ask yourself two questions:

1. What are they telling me?

2. What aren't they telling me?

You have a place, a date, a starting time and a name. The bare minimum information you need to simply turn up on the day. Leave it like that and you have uncertainty. What pieces in the jigsaw are missing?

Who is this mysterious Mr. Smith? You might assume he's the person they've designated to conduct the meeting. Assume nothing. Stories are legion of the unprepared turning up, being greeted by a 'Mr. Smith' who's only function is to lead them, as lambs to the slaughter, to an office in which resides a panel of inquisitors. Not being psyched up for a panel, and not knowing who these individuals are, can seriously disturb your mental equilibrium before getting your coat off. Surprises like this are both unnecessary and avoidable. It's inconceivable you would go to any other business meeting without having clarity on who would be present. *It's a sales meeting and you must know - to whom are you selling?* You have a right to know and a need to know. This information alone will inform and influence what you say and how you say it. Always be prepared for the goal posts to move at the last moment because you may have to think on your feet. For example, you may have turned up prepared to ask the buyer(s) a specific question about their department but if that morning the CEO decided on a whim to sit in on the meeting (yes, it does happen) then that really changes the dynamic - would it be wise to ask that question in the CEO's presence?

You'll always be given a starting time but rarely any indication of the scheduled duration - unless you request it. Don't assume that 'it'll take as long as it takes' or be content with some vague notion that it should take 'an hour or so.' Chances are high you'll be seen by someone inexperienced, unprepared and inclined to waste the first twenty minutes telling you his life story. He will then realise that time's running out, make heroic efforts to ask you some meaningful questions about your suitability for the role but then, ten minutes later, start winding it up by saying "Ok, I've got someone else to see now. Thank you for coming – I've enjoyed talking to you (which is all he's done), we'll be in touch."

So, that was a meeting only scheduled to last thirty minutes, twenty of which were wasted, and you leave without having sold a thing. If you clarify this before the meeting and establish that only thirty minutes has been allocated then at least you'll be psychologically prepared. What you can do about it? You can, on first meeting the other party, issue a gentle reminder - "Am I right that we have about half an hour?" A polite enough way of saying 'Get your skates on because I can't sell much in thirty minutes if you don't allow me to, so don't tell me your life story'. This is a good 'trigger' for him to get down to business and you must do it at the earliest opportunity, because once the hares start running and you're getting their life story it's more difficult, if not impossible, for you to turn it around. Again, the goal posts can move at the last minute – "It was half an hour but we've had a cancellation so we can go on longer if necessary'". Calling beforehand and seeking guidance on the timing often elicits, quite voluntarily, further information about your competition and the pecking order. This is 'nice to know' rather than 'need to know' information but the more pieces of the jigsaw you hold the better.

Knowing the anticipated timing has two other benefits: it will *dictate your pace* during the meeting and it will help you to predict when the 'End Game' (page 202) might kick in. You're going to the meeting to make a sale - *you need to know how long you've got to make it*. Again, it's inconceivable that you would agree to any other business meeting without establishing how much time it was likely to take – you're busy and have your own diary to sort out. For the most part job seekers don't establish this because it doesn't matter – they don't have a job so it could take all day as far as they're concerned. Or if they do establish it they frame it badly with the lame and less than enthusiastic 'How long is it going to last?' rather than the more businesslike 'How much time has been allocated?'

Is there any written information about their problem - sometimes quaintly called a 'Job Description'? These purport to accurately describe the role but rarely do so. But, if one exists and you can encourage the buyer to send it to you prior to the meeting then you've more information than your competitors – that's just got to be an advantage.

What do you know about the buyer's organisation? It's expected that you ought to know something about their business - it shows initiative and courtesy. Yet this research doesn't have to be a cloak and dagger exercise. Using websites is fine but why not get them to send you something relevant but which may not be on their website? It matters not whether they say yes or no, in just asking the question you are already opening up a dialogue and making a friend at court. Don't ask them for information you could easily get elsewhere but there's sometimes information specific to their need that you could request. In any other business situation if you felt that the other party held some information they could send prior to the meeting surely you wouldn't hesitate to request it. The more up to date your information the better - check out their social media interactions, read their blog. What have previous customers said? Check out their competition.

This meeting may have been arranged through a recruitment firm in which case it is their job to furnish you with some of this information and remove uncertainty. Some do this very well and are highly professional but others leave much to be desired. When you ask them how much time the buyer has allocated for the meeting it will most likely go quiet for a couple of seconds and then they will say 'I'd allow for about an hour if I were you' or 'it's normally an hour'. They've just made that up.

Incidentally, the buyer may still be using that 20th Century word 'interview' but you resist. In any dialogue or correspondence with the buyer you refer to a 'meeting' – you'll feel better and as we now know it more accurately makes the point that it's a two-way process.

This is where that distinction (page 49) between the private and government/public sectors often shows. On being invited to a meeting for a government sector appointment you'll most likely be sent all the information you require; job description, names and titles of those attending, timings, background information on the organisation and even dates for subsequent meetings. This thoroughness is courteous and best practice. There are exceptions but you are unlikely to encounter this in the private sector.

The removal of uncertainty is about getting as complete a picture of the scenario as you can before turning up on the day. You may consider these actions to be marginal gains but they all add up; these meetings are tough enough as they are – you don't want any surprises. You are turning up to give a performance, you must know your lines and when the curtain goes up, the spotlight will be on you. You must know who is in the audience and have some idea as to when the curtain will come down because, as we shall see, exits are just as important as entrances.

Be a little more circumspect about removing uncertainty with the 'hidden' market. If you have achieved the meeting through networking or making a direct approach then it may be inappropriate to ask, for example 'how much time has been allocated?'

So - Communicate!

Selling yourself is no more than an exercise in communication and something we can all sharpen up on. We don't communicate when we should and we communicate sometimes when it would be wiser not to do so. Once a line of communication has been opened up the general rule, and one to which it's worth subscribing, is to keep it open. It's useful to see this in terms of a tennis match and throughout the process of self-marketing you should ask 'Who's got the ball?'

Having received the ball in the form of an invitation to a meeting it would be courteous and businesslike to return it by communicating that you would be pleased to attend. Here's an opportunity for you to score a few points and again 'make a friend at court'. This can be achieved with a simple phone call. Now going about this in the wrong way can easily result in your making an enemy rather than a friend. Simply ringing up and launching into your agenda is a sure fire way of doing it. Always give the other party the option of putting the phone down, e.g. "I'm ringing to confirm I'll be pleased to attend at

2pm on 13 May – there's some things I need to clarify but if it's not convenient I can call back later". If the other party gives the green light then fine - ask questions about anything you feel needs clarifying.

It's useful to have your 'need to know' questions in some semblance of order as you may feel it inappropriate to ask all of them. This is a fine call and only you can judge the right moment to end the conversation. If you sense that you're really hitting it off with the other person you can sometimes get down to the small talk, e.g. "I guess you had a lot of applications for the position?" can get them to reveal how many applied and how many of those they are seeing. Again, you don't need this information but it's nice to know what you're up against. The crucial questions are those regarding whom you'll be seeing and the timing of the meeting - anything else is a bonus.

Having knocked the communication ball over the net you wouldn't expect any further communication before the meeting - unless you got them to agree to send you any other information. But don't relax yet. Consider knocking another ball over the net i.e.

communicate in writing that you'll be pleased to attend. The advantage of a call is that it can, and often should be, followed up by a letter - an altogether more tangible communication:

'Further to your letter dated 25 April and our subsequent conversation/my subsequent discussion with your PA, I am writing to confirm that I will indeed be pleased to meet both yourself and Mrs. Brown at 2 p.m. on 13 May, and thank you for agreeing to send the Job Description, which I look forward to receiving'.

This acts as a reminder for them to send it and that you had the initiative to ask for it. *In these days of instant electronic communication letter writing has gone out of fashion somewhat but don't completely eschew the letter as a means of communication when selling yourself - it retains the benefits of being businesslike, intimate and classier.* It may also be viewed as eccentric so be guided by your own instinct on this - you don't want them to think you're a crank.

Speed is the great benefit of an email but we don't tend to craft emails as carefully as letters, and speed is not always necessary so don't sacrifice quality for it. On many occasions there won't be time for all this and it is not always appropriate but in some situations by taking these actions you may be demonstrating the very skills they are seeking. Also, *choosing the right medium* to communicate can be critical. For example, don't be too quick to answer your mobile phone - 'wrong time/wrong place'. *Listening* is in itself a (much underrated) form of communicating. As we shall see later there may be times when you won't want to communicate at all - silence can speak a thousand words.

By now you may be forgiven for thinking 'This is a real chore - do I really have to do this?' The short answer is 'No, you don't' but that's the point - successful self-marketing is about taking the time and trouble to do those things that'll make you stand out from the competition. You're setting up the meeting by, at this early stage, presenting the buyer with a body of evidence to suggest that you, and no other, is worth hiring. Looking at it another way, if you choose not to do these things you might, just might, be competing with someone who has, while you're left on the starting blocks; it will always be your call. Also, it would be cynical to see these things as no more than some kind of technique to give you an edge on your competitors – yes, they can certainly give you those marginal gains, but they are firmly based on common sense, courtesy towards the other party and professionalism. No professional sales person would turn up to a meeting with a potential customer without having done some homework, clarified whom they were meeting and how long it would take.

I stress again, and not for the last time, no two meetings are the same. They all have their own uniqueness - their own 'dynamics' - and likewise the circumstances leading up to the meeting are unique. What you say, how you say it, or whether you say it at all at one meeting may be very different to what you say, how you say it or whether you say it at all at any other meeting. Hard and fast rules rarely apply. *The actions you take to remove uncertainty will change from meeting to meeting.* You'll be using your judgment and instincts across a range of issues. 'Winning At Interview' is giving you tools to put in your locker – when and how you choose to use them is up to you. But for now, seize every opportunity to get your name up in neon lights. Follow the rest of the herd and you'll have a tough campaign just like them.

We shall see later that there is a strong correlation between enjoyment and performance. This is why job hunting should be fun. If you make it a chore then you will be no good at it. *You make it fun by seizing initiatives, being creative, proactive and developing the will to win.* You also need to accept that successful job hunting can be (it doesn't *have* to be) 97% 'rejection'. You might think that if you were getting that amount of rejection then you must be doing something wrong. Well, let's not entirely eliminate that possibility, but the reality is that not everyone, or indeed anyone, will want to buy everything, or indeed anything, you are selling at any given moment. That's no reflection on you - that's the way it is in any market so don't get down about it because it will sap your morale.

---------♦ ♦ ♦-----------

Having The Conversations With Yourself

In Building Block 5 we saw that to win this competition you must articulate your truth in the most persuasive manner with which you are comfortable. *You can only achieve this to a high degree of professionalism if you have already articulated it to yourself before turning up to the meeting.* Yes, it can drive you a bit crazy but 'having the conversations with yourself' is the very essence of your preparation because it too removes uncertainty. If you omit to do this then 'being in the zone' won't save you. Our 2 out of 10 competent buyers would expect you to turn up with a head full of good news to give them - a rich palette of colours that enable you to paint the pictures. They will offer you a large canvas on which to paint those pictures, by asking you the right questions in the right way. Our 8 out of 10 won't have such high expectations and will afford you few opportunities, in a limited amount of time, to do this. The canvas they provide will be very much smaller. 'Having the conversations with yourself' will help them (Building Block 8) to more easily gather together the facts and the evidence.

To illustrate this we can learn a lot from how skilled politicians paint their pictures when given a small canvas by the more assertive, interrogational type of media interviewer. Those interviewers try to pin them down by asking direct 'closed' questions. Now politicians don't much care for these questions because they only invite 'yes' or 'no' answers (have you ever heard a politician say 'yes' or 'no'?). They will therefore deftly (and sometimes not so deftly) side-step such questions, not always because they don't want to answer them, but because they need to get their message across, just as *you need to get your message across in what may be a very limited amount of time.* It follows then that you must have clarity on what your message is. Politicians, on the whole, know what their message is because they know their stuff, have been well briefed and have thought about it before turning up. In effect, *they have removed uncertainty*. They are also aware that closed questions don't allow them to 'paint the pictures' in the limited amount of 'airtime' allowed for them to influence an audience of millions. Far from it, closed questions often paint *them* into a corner. Skilled lawyers will ask 'open' questions when they want defendants to talk and perhaps incriminate themselves and they are not averse to asking closed questions when circumstances demand. It's no coincidence that so many politicians have a legal background.

So how do they make the most of these questions and get their message across? Sometimes by using a technique called 'bridging'. On hearing the question the politician will typically pause, perhaps only for a second, as this gives them time to think (or simply for dramatic effect), *reframe* the question and then 'bridge' by saying (and this is only one example of many):

"Well, of course the question we are really asking here is........." They then proceed to put the reframed question on the table, which they now go on to answer. Like much else on this subject there is an art to bridging; the reframed question has to be 'on topic' i.e. it must bear some relation to the question that was originally posed - 'off topic' and it lacks all credibility. The politician can reframe a question by simply adding a word, omitting a word, questioning a word, re-arranging words or coming at it from a different angle. It's worth adding that too much bridging and reframing can be counter-productive as it can alienate the interviewer and cause the politician to appear slippery, evasive, even sinister, so an adept politician will use it judiciously.

Substitute the word 'politician' for the word 'seller' in the above paragraphs and we can see more clearly how relevant it is to you:

1. Only 2 out of 10 buyers will ask you 'open questions'. These are well framed and often begin with 'how' or simply 'tell me more about that'. They give you opportunities to get your message across. They invite sensible, interesting discussion. They encourage you to add colour. They are not averse to asking closed questions either if the circumstances demand.

2. Our 8 out of 10 will ask a lot of 'closed' questions, not because they are trying to 'pin you down' but simply because they haven't thought about it before turning up. You have to help them manage and control the meeting by doing what the politicians do - not necessarily by 'bridging' but simply by

responding to a closed question as if it had been an open one. If you fail to do this you will leave the meeting having (a) been interrogated (b) come across as having no mind of your own and (c) left them with a monochrome picture on that small canvas.

3. Have the confidence to 'question the question'. Buyers don't just want 'answers to questions' - they want considered responses, so pausing (sometimes if only for dramatic effect) demonstrates that you are thinking about the question.

If you are asked a question and you are sitting there thinking 'What's the right answer?' you are most likely done for. In an instant you have put yourself in a vulnerable position. Unless of course it is a technical question *there are no 'right' answers*; there are *your* responses based on your intellect, experience and not least common sense. Yes, this takes confidence but that invariably comes with preparation. On the whole you get respect from people if you can demonstrate that you have a view on something (even if it conflicts with their view), are prepared to articulate it, and fight your corner with a smile on your face. Trust your instincts.

I am still astonished at how many otherwise professional people will swan along to a life-changing business meeting without having invested the hours and hours into 'having the conversations with themselves', and then wonder why it all went wrong. The real tragedy is that they are exactly the same people who would spend a whole weekend of their own time preparing for a presentation they have to give on behalf of their own employer. Effort in - rewards out.

Dead Zone One

Your arrival at the venue for the meeting, ideally ten minutes before the appointed time, can signal the beginning of unforeseeable events. This period of time, after your arrival but before the meeting gets under way, is of unpredictable length and indeterminate nature. For dramatic effect let's call it 'Dead Zone One' and that curtain has now gone up. You should now be giving a good impression to everyone you meet - receptionists and security staff can exercise much influence on the decision makers. Display civility and not servility. This is also as good a time as any to turn your mobile phone OFF.

People are making judgments about you as soon as you enter the Dead Zone but the two-way process is under way, so how do you feel about them? With your 'business hat' firmly on your head be observant and soak up information.

Are they organised? Did they know you were coming? Are they pleased to see you or do they give the impression they don't much care whether you turned up or not? Do they keep you waiting an inordinate length of time without explanation or apology? These meetings do have a notorious reputation for over-running. This is where some of your Building Blocks may come into conflict - you may be making negative judgments about their off-hand and casual treatment of you and this may cause you to lose sight of your objective. But if this is how they are treating you now then how will they treat you once you join them? Sure, you've no decision to make until you get the offer, but is it already time to exercise your power of veto?

What environment do they provide for their people? Don't be fooled by the 'corporate plumage'. The impressive display you might see in the more public areas is not necessarily duplicated elsewhere. This highlights the importance of your making a point of asking to see where you might be working (the 'End Game' page 202).

Is any business going on? Do they look successful? It's not always possible to get an accurate assessment of this - some successful organisations exude an air of quiet efficiency rather than scenes of frenetic activity, but if no phones are ringing and you see people idly chatting around the water cooler then take note - you don't want to board a sinking ship.

Has any literature or other material been deliberately left lying around for you to notice? This is no time for snoozing. Be alert. You may have had little notice and no time to do any meaningful research, but if the buyer knows you've been sitting in reception for ten minutes with a copy of their annual report on the coffee table, which they'd deliberately put there, or with their 'mission statement' ('Mission Statements' seem to be going out of fashion) emblazoned on the wall, then any excuses from you that you've had no time to prepare for their question 'What do you know about us?' or 'What's our Mission Statement?' will have them reaching for the smelling salts. What have you been doing – staring out of the window?

What's their style? Look at the people you see coming and going. Do they look happy to be working there? Listen to conversations. If you see someone who's clearly a senior executive speaking with a junior member of staff, what is the tone and manner of that conversation - friendly or autocratic? How does it *feel*?

Strange things can happen in Dead Zone One – one seller was in the cloakroom and overheard this conversation between two executives: "Have you got a busy day?" 'Yes – I've got to interview this guy in ten minutes – I need that like I need a hole in the head – I haven't even read his CV yet.' Don't let this put you off making a visit - you can tell a lot by the condition of their cloakroom.

PA's / Receptionists are important people and human beings so treat them well. They can, and do, exert a lot of influence on decision makers and won't always wait to be asked – they may readily volunteer feedback (for better or worse) on your manner and behaviour. Good feedback from them will rarely change a negative decision the buyer may have made but it can reinforce a positive decision. Bad feedback from them can overturn a positive decision.

It's possible that your concentration on the above matters will serve to make you quite unaware of the buyer standing patiently over you trying to get your attention. They appear from nowhere. You are about to leave Dead Zone One and it's now show time.

---------♦ ♦ ♦---------

Chapter Three
42 Questions - The Answer To Everything

So - Why Should I Hire You?

We'd like to believe that these meetings are more than just question and answer sessions, but the reality is that the buyer asks questions, you respond accordingly and judgments are made on those responses. Of course you can't predict every question that might come up, but a good 80% are very predictable indeed – the same old chestnuts show up time and again, perhaps dressed up differently but sure enough - it's the same question with the same hidden agendas. There really is a limit to the number of questions you can ask the seller at these meetings. As the seller your success lies in your ability to anticipate the questions, analyse and interpret them accurately and have the conversations with yourself.

In this Chapter there are 42 generic questions. You will of course be able to think of many more that are germane to the problem you are turning up to discuss. *It matters not whether you actually get them*, but thoroughly prepare for them and not much will faze you at any meeting you attend. Your preparation for these questions will help you to have those conversations with yourself and give you the answer to everything. They will help you to marshal the facts and ensure that you turn up to any meeting with a head full of good news to deliver and a few defensive strategies to deploy. They are the words, sentences and phrases - the rich and sometimes subtle colours with which you will paint your pictures and thus get your message across.

In previous chapters I have on occasions mentioned that you are going to give a performance that is not entirely unlike being an actor going on stage - just to give a sense of drama and theatre. Well, this is where we must allow that analogy to break down because actors have a script - they have *lines to deliver*. You will not. Feeling that you have 'lines' to recite is not helpful and 'having the conversations with yourself' is not about you being a slave to some kind of script. No, I strongly recommend that you liberate yourself from that idea and give yourself the freedom to improvise - to go 'off-piste'. You may apply your colour sparingly; you may lay it on thickly, or not at all. There are also shades of grey. It will all hang on your perception of the buyer's problem and the chemistry between you. In effect you never paint the same picture twice and yet it will always be an accurate picture of you (Building block 5). Where do you start? In Building Block 7 we established that you are a 'probable' or at worst a 'possible'- so if you've got the meeting it's within your gift to convert it to an offer providing you can sell what you've turned up to sell and have some prepared strategies to overcome objections. We could rustle up more questions than we can shake a stick at so at first this might seem tricky, even daunting, but let's apply a little logic because there are, in a sense, only 2 questions for you to consider! One of them you want and the other you most certainly don't want.

Why should they hire me? These are the ones you love and really want them to ask you. They are not inherently dangerous. They are all opportunities to sell something and the worst you can do is waste them. These are the 'knock 'em for six' questions. 'Paint the pictures' and you will win the prize.

Why wouldn't they hire me? You haven't turned up to the meeting to answer these. The best you can do is 'keep a straight bat'. *You can't sell anything* off the back of these questions. They are 'objections to the sale' – hence the need for defensive strategies; and this is where your ability to 'bridge' and 'reframe' may come in useful (page 67).

Yes, it really is as simple as that. Just about any question you might care to think of will fall into one of the above categories. Your success depends upon your ability to distinguish the 'sell' questions from the 'defend' ones. Question 1 above is the only question you've turned up to answer. They are blank cheques – fill 'em in. Go unprepared and you'll leave the meeting having wasted more time on question 2, and given the buyer more reasons why you shouldn't be hired.

Let's limber up and test the theory. Here's a selection of the predictable questions, some of them are clichés and thus 'tired' and some I have 'framed' badly e.g. 'closed' questions. This is quite deliberate

(Building Block 8), and an intelligent question framed well is always easier to deal with than a dumb question framed badly. Each is denoted by the symbol [+] or [-]. The questions [+] are the seductive 'Why should they hire me?' questions. The others, denoted [-] are the potentially dangerous 'Why wouldn't they hire me?' questions and are inviting you to shoot yourself in the foot. They require deft handling and evasive action as any one of them can bring this blind date to a tearful conclusion.

'How was your journey?' [+]

Mostly harmless, but even this seemingly innocuous icebreaker can be turned by the unguarded into a [-] question. A bore is someone who, when you ask them how they are, really tells you. This question falls into the same category. There's no overt hidden agenda but even if you've had the journey from hell, resist the temptation to say so. They'll likely conclude that if you're going to have that problem at the beginning and end of every day then they may as well not hire you. You may be tempted to reach the same conclusion, in which case you have already forgotten Building Block 3 – not a good start. You might consider selling your planning skills by saying 'Fine - I took the precaution of checking it out beforehand.' Don't - that's over-selling before you've even got your coat off. This question can make an early appearance during 'Dead Zone One'. Don't tell them your journey was a breeze if it wasn't. That demonstrates that you've also forgotten Building Block 5. The greatest sin you can be guilty of is the sin of omission. *Don't tell anyone anything they don't need to know.*

'Tell me about yourself' [+]

This won't come half way through the meeting but will most likely hit you as soon as you've sat down. This isn't generally recognised as being a great way to begin one of these meetings but as most buyers are ill prepared this might account for its frequency. *If you get this you can be fairly certain that this buyer is going to need your help* (Building Block 8). Perversely, it's a terrific question to get, but only if you are prepared for it. Because it will come at the beginning and not half way through the meeting it assumes an importance above all other questions as your response sets the standard for the rest of the meeting. Respond well and your confidence will soar; you will have laid a solid foundation on which to build. Begin badly and you'll know it, thus sending your confidence into freefall. It also sets the standard for your competitors, as the chances are high that they too will encounter it.

Failure to prepare for 'tell me about yourself' almost guarantees that one of three things will happen:

You may be tempted to ask the buyer to clarify the question. Don't do that. There's no advantage in your doing so. Never assume that buyers know why they are asking this or indeed any other question. It's more likely that the buyer is really saying; " I'm unprepared for this meeting and have no structure or agenda so I'll tell you what - you start and we'll see where the conversation takes us." If you ask "what do you want to know?" they'll be forced to pluck something out of the ether which might not be in your interests but about which you now have to talk; you're already out of control. Only a poor salesman would respond to the question "Tell me about your product" with "What do you want to know?" A good salesman would seize it as the opportunity to explain why you can't afford *not* to buy the product.

Secondly, you'll make heroic efforts to deal with it but without having had this conversation with yourself it will all wither on the vine after about thirty seconds. You'll have started badly, *wasted what is a great question to get* and feel embarrassed about it. Your body language will all too visibly convey that your cupboard is bare and the buyer will have to come to the rescue in an effort to breathe some new life into the meeting. You may not have done any damage – there's a limit to how much damage you can do in thirty seconds, but you'll have sold nothing and lowered the bar, right from the off.

Finally, it may be your nervous reaction to start talking and not know when to stop. By the end of 15 minutes you'll have presented the buyer with a long rambling discourse of irrelevant, disjointed and damaging information and have no idea what supplementary questions might follow. You can do a lot of damage in 15 minutes. Sellers also have an alarming habit of bringing their emotional baggage to these meetings and dumping it in the buyer's lap at the first opportunity, and 'Tell me about yourself' [+] provides the perfect opportunity because it's such a broad question. It's quite amazing how many people begin their response by telling the buyer how old they are. You may feel vulnerable about your age but why put it on the table? Buyers are more likely to have a problem with it once sellers indicate that *they* see it as an issue. An opening statement like "Well, I'm 55 years old..." is really sending the signal 'I'm 55 years old and if you've got a problem with that let's get it on the table now.'

Before the meeting always assume you'll get this question. You *want* it because it's the archetypal 'Why should I hire you?' question. Look carefully at your understanding of their need. Be objective and ask yourself 'Well - why should they hire me?' 'What can I bring to their party?' Remember Building Block 7. They must, at the very least, believe that you could possibly be the right person; otherwise they wouldn't be wasting their time. What's attracted them? Identify these things, make a list and formulate a response around them. Write it all out, refine it, read it aloud, time it. Not many people can engage the buyer's attention on this for more than 3 minutes, so 2 minutes is about right – you can sell a lot of good things in 2 minutes provided you are focused. As content is critical we won't be obsessive about '2 minutes' – the buyer would rather get one minute of good, clear, relevant information than two minutes of what could still be waffle. Set 'milestones' for yourself and carve up your response into manageable sections of say, 30 seconds each. So, if you go for two minutes *identify four relevant things about yourself* that you would like to get on the table at the beginning of the meeting. On completion look at it again and take it a stage further. Ask yourself 'If I say these things what supplementary questions might they come up with?' It doesn't require a great deal of creativity and imagination to then ask yourself 'Well, what supplementary questions would I *want* them to come up with?' With sound preparation you can decide the direction in which you want the meeting to go. You can actually tempt the buyer into *asking you the question you would rather get,* not the one that will arise as the result of an off-the-cuff remark from you.

Received wisdom has it that buyers should be in control of the meeting; it is after all taking place on their territory and at their behest. To an extent this is correct but as a prepared seller you can exert a high degree of influence and subtlety that allows you to direct the course of the discussion, but not in such a way that you wrest control from the buyer. So, look again at your 'four things' and identify one of them that is a 'furrow worth ploughing'. Take this approach with each one as they may interject at any time, but this is the one you *want* the buyer to drill down on and ask supplementary questions about. It will be the most *relevant* thing about yourself and the topic you believe they'll be most interested in. It is perhaps your most vivid colour. Now, *deliberately make it point four*. Given that eight times out of ten a supplementary question will arise as result of the last thing they heard you talking about it makes sense to save your juiciest morsel till last. If you choose this topic well then the buyer will recognise it as being highly relevant and want to drill down on it. But you can help them to ask you the questions you'd rather get. For example, your final few seconds might be: "It was a challenging project and presented some major problems, but I enjoyed it and learned a lot from the experience. So, that's a brief summary of me and my background." Now, if you've chosen your final topic well the buyer would want to stick with it and should be tempted to fall on that like a dog on a bone as you are deliberately provoking the supplementary [+] questions:

'What were those challenges and how did you meet them?'

'What problems and how did you solve them?'

'What specific aspects of the role did you particularly enjoy and why?'

'What did you learn?'

But if you had referred to the problems without thinking then it might now be a [-] question and you'd be fighting a rearguard action. These are all 'hooks' that you deliberately weave into your narrative and yes, it is manipulative but for all the right reasons; you are helping the inexperienced buyer to focus on what you see as the key issue. Preparing for the above supplementary questions enables you to rise head and shoulders above your competitors. If they are prepared at all they will typically give a very thin historical monochrome narrative of *what* they have done, which is less than helpful to the buyer. Deliberately provoking the supplementary questions invites them to dig much deeper, go way beyond 'what you have done' and ask *how and why* you did things - that's much more *behavioural*. It gives the meeting more breadth, depth and scope.

One great virtue of preparing a response is that you'll know where the full stop is at least meant to be. Another advantage is that with subsequent meetings for other roles you don't have to keep re-inventing the wheel by preparing a new response from scratch. It will just require some fine-tuning. Note the use of the word 'enjoyed'. There's a strong correlation between 'enjoyment' and 'performance' and a correlation that many buyers will draw, albeit subliminally. It is an uplifting word to hear - it is 'good news' so never leave a meeting without having used it in some context. It is very telling, and telling by its absence, how many sellers leave a meeting without having told the buyer that they *enjoy* their work. In itself it might not stop them from hiring you but it's an unnecessary omission.

You may be tempted to structure your response by talking the buyer historically through your CV. This may work well for you but the more experience we have and the more years we have to cover the less effective this tends to be, as there's likely to be too much irrelevant information to get through. And, just for you old guys out there, the buyer's eyes will glaze over if you begin wistfully with: "Well, when I left college in 1987 " - ('Oh no, don't start there, it's 2017 and we only have an hour – get a move on'). Or, as one buyer memorably interjected: 'Can you please move on and bring me into the 21st century?' Selecting 4 relevant selling points from your experience allows you to escape from that historical straightjacket.

It's important that you do what works for you but find a confident way to begin your response. For example: "Well, I'll have to be a bit selective so I'll just touch on some of those *things* about myself *and my background* that, having read your job description, will be of interest to you". The buyer will know immediately that you've come prepared, be thankful that you're going to be selective and happy that you're now about to tell them something interesting. They will also know that all they have to do is relax, sit back and make notes while you spend 2 minutes adding to their shopping list and giving them good news. And they will love you for it. Note also how that confident introduction reframes the question (page 67) simply by adding the word 'background' - it broadens out the scope of what you can now tell them. Note also the use of the more generic word 'things' - try not to use 'interview' language e.g. 'skills', 'competencies'.

Don't let your head drop if they start the meeting in any other way. Just preparing for 'tell me about yourself" makes you focus on the 4 most relevant things you're selling and how to sell them. You will turn up with those colours in your head and apply them at some point during the meeting, perhaps not in one 2-minute coverage but 30 seconds here and 30 seconds there, plus the additional colour you have prepared in response to those supplementary questions.

Building Block 8 is most relevant here because it helps to establish as soon as possible if you are sitting in front of one of those 2 from 10 trained buyers or 8 from 10 untrained and inexperienced buyers. If they have chosen a comfortable and relaxing setting then that, by itself, doesn't necessarily mean they have been trained. It could simply mean that that's where they've decided to do it. But if they are sitting behind a desk, start with 'tell me about yourself', don't explain their problem, ask a lot of closed or badly framed questions, don't drill down on your responses by requesting examples, and give you the impression that they haven't invested much of their time into preparing for this meeting then they are going to need your help.

Your CV – it's all hype isn't it? [-]

Oh yes – you meet some interesting characters out there. Those wham, bam shoot from the hip no nonsense types who won't start a meeting with the warm, touchy feely 'Tell me about yourself'. Oh no, the 'shock and awe' approach before you've warmed your seat is what floats their boat. This would destroy the less confident but don't panic! Why? Well, if the buyer really believed your CV to be all 'hype' you wouldn't be there would you? This caveman is really saying 'Look, I've given your CV the benefit of the doubt but it could be complete fiction for all I know and I'm a busy person, so if you're selling snake oil I won't want to hire you - so confess now.' This is an example of how our 'Two Guiding Principles' of truth and supportability (Building Block 5)) can be severely tested - don't be found wanting.

With any luck your competitors will allow themselves to be bludgeoned into submission by this Neanderthal. You, on the other hand, will stay cool, calm and collected, look mildly surprised, raise an eyebrow, maybe even crack a smile (a smile can be very disarming) and respond with "No, no hype – show me some hype and I'll back up my CV."

A statement on your CV such as 'Strong team building skills' begs the obvious question 'What are they?' Such questions are [+] but only if you can support your statements with firm evidence. Be ready for the supplementary questions: ('*How* strong are they?', '*How* do you measure team building skills?' and 'Who told you that?'). This question and the way it is framed is an instant and robust challenge to test your CV for credibility and your ability to remain calm under pressure. Rise to it.

You should have specifically designed, structured, fashioned and polished your sales literature to provoke questions. *You must know what questions it is provoking*. It's potentially the agenda for the meeting and you have set it. Lose credibility on one word and your whole CV tumbles like a pack of cards.

What do you know about us?   [+]

What you know is probably less important than being able to display that you've taken the trouble to find out something about them. It sells initiative and courtesy. It's really impressive if you can tell them something *they* don't know but that's more a matter of luck than judgment. If they have retail outlets/branches/premises that you could visit as a customer prior to the meeting then it's critical that you do so, otherwise you can really come unstuck:

'When you were last in one of our branches what impressed you?' [+]

And 'Did you notice anything you think we could improve on?' [-]

If you have to hold up your hands and admit you haven't bothered to check them out then most will allow the meeting to run its course, because on the whole they are courteous people, but in their thoughts you've now been sent for an early bath. With [-] don't be too critical. You may be talking to the person whose remit it is, or if there are two or more buyers at the meeting one of them may be responsible for that part of the business you are criticising - you can make an enemy without knowing it. It's generally expected that sellers will have done their homework and failure to do so can turn a 'probable' into a 'possible' or knock you out of the game entirely if the buyer sees it as a killer question.

Don't expect all buyers to ask this question. If they don't you could easily leave the meeting without having sold the fact that you'd done your homework. So with preparation you could 'weave it in' (page 119) to your response to 'Tell me about yourself' or sell it during the 'End Game' (page 202).

Why does this job interest you? [+]

Their problem can interest you for many valid reasons and you'd normally be quite safe laying any of them on the table. Avoid clichés like the plague; now there's nothing wrong whatsoever with a 'challenge', but voice it in response to this question and you may just detect an audible whimper–it's a sign that you're bereft of any real ideas. Why might they want it to interest you? Presumably because of what you can bring to it in terms of skills, experience and perhaps personal qualities - try to place the emphasis on these 'below the line' (Building Block 1) things and not so much on what you can get from it e.g. 'challenge', 'career progression'. This is an opportunity for you to 'make the match' and impress on them that you're the solution to their problem. How can you make a difference?

Remember - you haven't turned up to get a job. *The more you drill down on their problem the more likely it becomes, far more likely, that you are the one who is asked to solve it. Stay 'in the zone'.*

Why are you leaving? [-]

Hidden agenda - 'Are you leaving/did you leave for any reasons that might stop me from hiring you?' The buyer may not realise this is the hidden agenda but the wrong response from you will reveal it. In pure recruitment terms there's only one valid reason for leaving one organisation and joining another - to broaden our experience. In reality we all understand that there's other reasons why we move - some more acceptable than others. Many of us find ourselves in the market for work as a result of change e.g. restructuring, downsizing, cost cutting (all those 'below the line ' reasons) and no sensible buyers would have a problem with it. Unfortunately, sellers do themselves a real disservice by the way in which they express it. The cardinal sin is to simply say 'I was made redundant' or 'I was fired'. Study it closely and you'll see there's something pathetic about it. It's the seller as 'victim' *and they don't want to meet a victim.* The 'I' word takes ownership of the word 'redundancy', which is a shame as it belongs to your previous organisation, not you. Such an answer therefore is both negative and misleading. It sends the following signals:

- The seller and no others were selected for redundancy. This is rarely the case.

- The seller is a 'job beggar' (Building Block 1).

- There's more to 'uncover' about this redundancy.

'I've been made redundant' will almost certainly lead to a litany of supplementary questions, many of which are **[-]** but at best are wasting time. For 'Human Resource' specialists redundancy is the sticky part of their role and they will, *if you give them the opportunity*, show a real interest in it, e.g. 'that must have been a shock? **[-]**', 'How do you feel about it? **[-]**', 'How well do you think your organisation handled it? **[-]**'.

This is no time to pour your heart out so there's no mileage in these supplementary questions; it's far better to close it down in such a way that the buyer will be reassured, lose interest and move on to the more [+] questions. Here's how to help them do that:

Structure a response with three parts to it, a beginning, middle and an end:

Part 1

Give the buyers a time frame to indicate that it was all part of an ongoing process e.g. 'Over the past year'. This lets them know from the start that you didn't have to leave as the result of some overnight 'knee jerk' decision where, for all they know, you could have got caught with your hand in the cookie jar. Now use the word 'change' and/or 're-structuring' 'there's been a lot of re-structuring'. This is a concept they are familiar with and their interest is already waning. Don't give your opinion on it - opinions can be dangerous so don't let the word 'unfortunately' creep in – a victim word that has baggage.

Part 2:

Tell them what the result of that change/restructuring has been in terms of the number of *jobs* (not 'people') that have been affected

'During this period thirty jobs have gone and mine is one of them'. This gives them the big picture, and the truthful one (Building Block 5) because jobs are made redundant - not people. Make sure that the 'unfortunately' word doesn't creep in here either as in 'unfortunately mine is one of them' as it sends the signal 'the only reason I'm sitting here today talking to you is because I've been on the receiving end of misfortune.' In such ways do we present ourselves as 'victims', but don't stop talking here though as those time - wasting supplementary **[-]** questions are still queuing up.

Part 3: Now end on a high note. A note of optimism, enthusiasm and of the future rather than the past e.g. 'I've really enjoyed my previous role but this is a great opportunity to use my skills in an organisation like yours'. This tells them that you feel just fine about the whole debacle thus preventing them from asking you. Now encourage them to ask a 'Why should I hire you?' question: 'I believe I've a lot to offer'. The supplementary question 'What *have* you got to offer?' **[+]** is now virtually irresistible and providing you are prepared then this will be a road along which you're more than happy to travel. And you will of course be prepared because 'What have you got to offer?' is 'Tell me about yourself' dressed up differently. So, if it hadn't been asked at the beginning you've made it turn up now. On the whole buyers are not used to meeting sellers who've come prepared to say what they have to offer so there's a strong intrigue factor here.

Brevity is important with [-] questions. The more words you offer up the greater the danger of inviting supplementary [-] questions that get you bogged down. It should take no more than twenty seconds to kill this time-wasting question stone dead. It's worth emphasising that no one you'll meet will have a problem with issues like redundancy. Far from it – most of the buyers will have been touched by it themselves at some time so the empathy value is high. But it's that very empathy that can cause the problem, as you don't want to segue into swapping war stories with the buyer (You think *that* was bad? Let me tell you what they did to me!). It's just that *you can't sell anything* off the back of this question so those supplementary questions simply waste valuable selling time. The importance of body language cannot be overstated as words on the printed page are one thing, but there must be synergy between your words and your body language, so if you didn't enjoy your last job then don't say that you did, as your body language won't convey that and you would be breaking our guiding principles; but they would much prefer to hear good news.

These are only examples to demonstrate the strategy and you will of course put your own imprint on these to truthfully reflect your situation and feelings. If you are attempting to make a career transition for example then that's often a difficult 'sell' and you may choose to conclude Part 3 with 'This has given me time to take stock and *understand my transferable skills.*' This begs the question 'What are they?' [+].

Why is making a career change, however slight, such a difficult 'sell'? Well, particularly in the 'visible' and much more competitive market i.e. job advertisements and agencies*, you will invariably need some kind of 'bridgehead' to gain entry. Studying for a qualification may be your 'bridgehead' or it can come in the form of a 'transferable asset', a skill, knowledge, experience or combination of all of them. 'You don't have any experience in this sector so how can you make the transition?' [-] can be forestalled and confidently dealt with using this strategy. It doesn't normally pay to defend an objection before it is voiced but with such an obvious objection as this the risk is small; and as we shall see later, not all objections *are* voiced (our 8 out of 10 don't always have the confidence to articulate their truth) so you can't afford to leave a meeting with this particular elephant still in the room. Weave your transferable asset(s) into your narrative somehow - it's your ticket to get in, and a seemingly throwaway line like: ' I have some good transferable skills' is saying: 'I'm up for talking about this so you may now ask me what they are'. Should you leave a meeting saying to yourself 'What a stroke of luck - they didn't ask me about my lack of experience in their sector!' then you are most likely being delusional.

* When 'jobs' are advertised the buyers are looking for 'round pegs for round holes' i.e. someone to

neatly fit a role. If you don't neatly fit it's difficult to gain entry. They won't squeeze you in. Doors open more readily in the 'hidden' market i.e. networking and direct approaches, as they often have a more open mind and you are not competing with anyone.

Why did you stay with them for so long? [-]

This is an implied criticism, with the not so hidden agenda that you suffer from inertia, are uncomfortable with change and have no ambition to progress. Staying with the same employer for the whole of our working life 'womb to tomb' used to be very much the norm. It showed commendable qualities such as commitment and loyalty. For some it was the perfect vehicle for a rewarding career. For many more it provided no more than a welcome security blanket. Now that employers have taken their blankets back we're hung out to dry in the chill wind of an ever-changing market place populated by 'buyers' and 'sellers'. Well, that's change, and that's progress. Fortunately for us, 'change' and 'progress' are the keys to this question. If there's evidence to show that you didn't stand still then you must put it on the table and defend yourself against this unfair accusation "I was there 20 years because they were a great company to work for and, as you'll see from my CV, I wasn't getting the same experience twenty times over." We need not necessarily be talking about promotion here. A succession of different roles at the same level is enough and is in its own way progression. "I always felt I was making a positive contribution to the business and giving added value". This begs the follow up questions: 'What value did you add to your last role?' [+], 'What added value can you bring to this role?' [+] 'What contribution can you make to our business?' [+].

I'll wager that this is also your truth - " I *feel* as if I've worked for four different organisations. They're not the same business today that I joined 20 years ago". Then you might want to expand on this and talk about those changes (i.e. mergers, takeovers, expansion, diversification etc) and how you helped them through those transitions.

As we've already seen 'Endings' are really quite important, because invariably the supplementary questions will arise from the *last* thing the buyer heard you say. Taking care over what you're going to say and how you're going to say it can pay real dividends but retain the courage to veer 'off script'.

A word of caution: The phrase "As you'll see from my CV…" must be used sparingly. Some sellers appear to be umbilically attached to their CV and constant repetition of the phrase gets tiresome. If you have gone to a lot of trouble to write your CV (which of course you have because it must be the best example of the written work you are capable of producing) and the buyers don't seem to show much interest in it then yes, that can be frustrating, but be prepared to cut it loose and let it go. You've set it as the agenda for the meeting but you can't make them use it. Incidentally, those two out of ten trained buyers who have *studied* your CV may, if they want to be mischievous or test your tact, diplomacy, patience - and not least your truthfulness, deliberately ask you a question, the answer to which is plain to see on that CV, just to see how you react. If you visibly bridle in the face of such questions the meeting may slowly grind to a halt.

You've done a lot of job-hopping - why? [-]

The hidden agendas here may be that you haven't found your niche in life; you lack commitment; you can't hold down a role for any reasonable length of time; you don't get on with people; you're unreliable if not feckless. If these are all true of course then you've got your work cut out, but it's not necessary for you to explain, and least of all apologise for, each change you've made. If the changes you made allowed you to broaden your experience then say so:

"Ideally I'd prefer to progress within the same organisation, but so far, to broaden my experience, I've had to take the initiative to achieve that. For example..." Now give an example of a good career move, explain the rationale behind it and leave it at that. In these times of constant and unremitting change buyers don't really expect anyone to stay with them for the whole of their working lives, and yet they invariably expect sellers to send 'commitment' signals, which suggest they might do just that. This is an example of the necessary role-playing highlighted in Building Block 4.

What is your greatest strength? [+]

This is a tired question but nonetheless it's a gift so grab it with both hands. Interpret this as 'Give me one reason why I should hire you?' It's amazing how many sellers make the mistake of dumping a hatful of strengths into the buyers lap, to share and enjoy, but are marked down because of their failure to interpret the question accurately. 'Greatest' implies 'one strength only, please'.

The worst you can do with this question is waste it and it's very much wasted if you sell a strength they don't want to buy, so make it relevant. It's most unlikely that anyone will frame the question as 'What's your greatest strength *relevant* to solving our problem?' They'll simply say 'what's your greatest strength?' and then hope and pray you offer something that they actually want to buy. So there's no advantage in selling irrelevancies. In preparing your response do have this conversation with yourself: 'Based on my understanding of their problem, what would they *want* my greatest strength to be?' If you can identify it and it happens to *be* your greatest strength then that's a happy coincidence. If it's your third greatest strength there's little merit in selling either of the first two, and the question itself is somewhat specious, for how do you measure strengths on a scale of one to ten? As long as it is a strength you possess and can support then you are not compromising on Building Block 5. You may choose to come up with a strength that might compensate for a weakness you expect them to probe at some point. For example, if the role will require you to change your established pattern of work, perhaps moving into a different sector, then you might be wise to sell your 'adaptability' - sell this early on and it has much credibility should they raise the objection later, as you can refer back. Don't sell something that you can't support as this isn't helpful to anyone (Building Block 5).

Ensure you have at least two examples to back up whatever you choose to sell as your greatest strength. Most likely you'll only need one but someone of a more probing, mischievous or downright awkward disposition might say 'give me another one' - their rationale being that if that's your greatest strength then you really ought to have more than one example to back it up, and who are we to argue? Examples and anecdotes are essential pieces of ammunition to take along to these meetings as they give credence to what you are saying; they are the *evidence* to support your strengths and attributes and they demonstrate how you behaved/performed in previous situations – a useful indicator as to how you would perform in the role being discussed - the very rationale behind competency-based meetings. Without them you can be sunk, and don't always wait to be asked for them - poorly prepared and inexperienced buyers (Building Block 8) won't always ask for examples, thus depriving you of an opportunity to convince them. If you judge that the buyer is inexperienced and needs a lot of help then you wouldn't be helping if you simply said "My greatest strength is my adaptability" as the chances are they'll just move on to the next question which, as sure as night follows day, is likely to be 'and what is your greatest weakness?' More helpful to say: "My greatest strength is my adaptability. *For example…*"

When selling your experience don't plough too narrow a furrow i.e. harvest your examples from as wide a field as possible as it gets across the scope of your experience and gives a meeting breadth, depth and that vital colour. From the buyers perspective it can get tiresome hearing about the same project or role from which you seem to be drawing all your examples and anecdotes. Get all the selling points you can from any one experience but have the courage to take your bucket to different wells and draw from them. Don't risk losing their attention and make them think 'haven't you done anything else?' Examples drawn from non-work experiences can have great validity as they can sell transferable skills, knowledge, experience or other attributes.

Consistency is a useful and revealing 'tool' of 'interviewing', which isn't used as often as it should be, unsurprisingly given Building Block 8. But a perceptive buyer will expect to see consistency in your responses, to sometimes seemingly different questions, throughout a meeting or across two or more meetings. You may well be asked for your greatest strength at both the first and any subsequent meetings - they wouldn't want it to be any different at the second time of asking. For this reason alone the first thing you must do *immediately* after the meeting (don't wait until you get home to do this. It's surprising how much of a meeting can dissipate from your mind in only 30 minutes) is make some notes. The next meeting may not be for three weeks or more and to refresh your memory you must have a record of the first meeting to which you can refer. Now that you've prepared for 'What is your greatest strength?' you can now see how it won't matter if the question doesn't come up – you've got some good news to give about yourself – you've 'locked on' to it and it's planted in your brain. Trust that you will articulate it at the meeting one way or another, and if you think that was a tough question you may want to look away now.

What is your greatest weakness? [-]

This is a monster and the archetypal 'Tell me why I shouldn't hire you' question. Well now, if the meeting has until this point progressed in a satisfactory manner then the match is being made, in which case buyers really don't want sellers to shoot themselves in the foot. Unfortunately most sellers do just that by volunteering a weakness relevant to the role being discussed. When this happens the buyer's heart sinks because it can't be ignored, and they were that close to believing they'd found the solution to their problem. It's often preceded by the previous question which gives you time to mentally get it lined up in your sights, but it can come right out of the blue.

As this is such a loaded question it's advisable to have four possible lines of defence, any one of which you might call upon depending on your judgment of the buyer's manner, personality and not least sense of humour, or lack of it.

Plan A

Humour does have a role to play and can sometimes defuse a tricky situation. It can also be perceived as flippancy, sarcasm or even hysteria, so proceed with caution. The simple riposte 'chocolate' has got many a seller out of this difficulty, providing the accompanying body language is non-confrontational. It also helps if the accompanying body is not overly corpulent. Reading this in cold print you may have some doubts about how effective such a response might be but judge it right and it'll work in your favour more often than you might think. To understand why this might be we only have to remind ourselves of one incontrovertible truth about these meetings: BUYERS' DON'T WANT TO HEAR BAD NEWS. This is one of the great paradoxes of the buyer/seller relationship. When the meeting is going well and the match is being made the buyer really doesn't want the seller to screw up. But they have a job to do and can't just ask the [+] questions. They have to go to places they don't particularly want to go. They have to ask the **[-]** 'give me bad news' questions, but they don't *want* bad news. If the match isn't being made and the chemistry/rapport is not good then Plan A is high risk. If you go for Plan A have faith in it and do give it time to work as it can take the buyer a second or two to decide to move on. Don't crank it up again by saying " …but seriously…"

Plan B

As the underlying question can be interpreted as 'do you have a weakness relevant to the role?' then there's sanctuary to be found in giving an irrelevant weakness. If for example you're selling skills that are primarily cerebral then admitting to a weakness of a practical nature shouldn't be damaging "I've been a driver for years, but the mysteries of the internal combustion engine have completely passed me by, but it's of no interest to me, if I break down I'd rather make a call." Now that's an extreme example simply to demonstrate the strategy and it's so important you bring your own imagination to bear on all of this - it's fun! If you seek more subtlety you might unearth something 'quasi-relevant' - a skill/experience/knowledge you lack but that is so way out on the periphery of the problem being discussed you're confident that for the buyer it won't be a deal breaker. Find a small bone on which they can have a nibble.

Plan C

Whether opting for Plans A, B, C or D you may choose to pause for a few seconds as if pole-axed and stare philosophically out of the window (now this is the time for chin-stroking) - by any standards it's a tough question and responding too quickly, even though the tape is running, can ruin the dramatic effect, so give them the impression that they have really got you on the ropes. As we now know, you are giving a performance and there are some occasions, and this is one of them, when you may need a bit of theatre. To show the buyer that you're trying to answer the question objectively your preamble can be "Well that's a tough question because we don't see ourselves as others see us (true enough) and then go on to sell what to the buyer is a strength ".... sometimes my wife/husband/partner accuses me of not getting the balance right between work and play", then agree with that accusation just a little ".... and I guess I should build more leisure time into my diary" now disagree with it just a little ".... but I enjoy my work"(you've just sold something!), now take some heat out of it ".... and we don't fall out over it." It's too crude and hackneyed to say, "I'm a workaholic". It's also dangerous as that's a real addiction and no organisation in their right mind would want a workaholic on their payroll. It's more compelling if you say that others accuse you of it because you're being objective not subjective. You can easily find variants of Plan C. For example, if 'attention to detail' is clearly a pre-requisite for solving their problem then "...sometimes I've been accused of paying too much attention to detail, (now put up a robust defence) but I've always found that to do this work successfully you have to dot the ' I ' s and cross the 't' s - I've worked with others who don't do this and they always come unstuck. But there you are – not everyone shares my view on that." Now if you've judged it right the buyer is thinking' Yes, I've worked with those people and I don't want to hire them - I want to hire you!' As part of your preparation have a look through any old appraisals or 360degree feedback and reappraise yourself of what other people *have* actually said of you (see page 160 'A Word About Humility'). You may find clues there to help with Plan C.

Plan D

Although it's never acceptable to say that you don't have any weaknesses it's entirely legitimate, in the heat of battle, to say "Right now I can't think of one and I do believe we build a job on our strengths not weaknesses" (but then answer the question historically) "...but, if you'd asked me that question only a year ago" (now give an example of something you weren't that good at a year back) "...I would have said that giving presentations to clients wasn't something I enjoyed" (now tell them what actions you took) "...but I had to get on with it and was really lucky because my boss was great at giving presentations and she gave me a lot of help. Now I'm good at it too and I enjoy it. I don't think weaknesses are a problem if we know what they are and do something about it." The great advantage with this is that the example you give can be relevant or irrelevant – as the seller you can't lose.

The above example has three other benefits. Firstly, giving presentations or speeches is something that scares the living daylights out of most people, so giving a weakness with a strong empathy value is all to the good. Secondly, it paints a picture of a good working relationship with the boss (see below). Giving credit to and flattering previous bosses will never fail to impress. Thirdly, with Plan C you, the seller, are choosing to use the 'competency based' rationale (that previous behaviour/performance is a good indicator of how you might behave today) by giving a *structured example* based on the STAR principle - you describe the **S**ituation (previous role), described the **T**ask (giving presentations) told them what **A**ction you took (working closely with your boss) and told them the **R**esult (now you are good at it).

Although you must have all four defensive strategies in your head you'll never need more than two of them at any given meeting. What plan you adopt might even depend on *when* the question is asked. For example, if it comes right at the start, before you've really sold anything and built that necessary rapport, and certainly if you are facing a buyer with no sense of humour, then you might be wise to abandon Plan A because it will go down like a concrete parachute - an hour later it might present very well.

Robust intro's to Plans B, C and D are "I believe we build a job on our strengths not our weaknesses but...." and " Well, I'm not sure how we measure weaknesses on a scale of one to ten but..." or "Well, to come up with a weakness I'd be really nitpicking but..."

A final reminder - you can't just make these things up. Do the self-analysis and identify your strengths, because that's what you are selling. But you must also know what you're weaknesses are. You may have a greatest weakness which, if put on the table at a meeting, wouldn't cause you a problem at all. Conversely, you may have a greatest weakness that could blow you out of the water if you offered it up at a meeting - in which case you have a decision to make.

---------♦ ♦ ♦---------

Weaving The Tapestry - The Subliminal Sell

Now here's as good a time as any to flag up an important 'dynamic' about the seller/buyer relationship. Selling yourself well at these meetings isn't solely about giving 'good' answers to some tricky questions. The real art is like weaving a tapestry where there are 'underlying threads' running through your narrative. Threads that allow you to sell subsidiary, yet often crucial, things that the buyers need to know, but which on the face of it have nothing to do with the question you have been asked. For example, all buyers are going to need to know what kind of a person you are to have around. Are you going to fit in? When buyers know they need to know it they will ask the open questions that take them there, perhaps by probing previous relationships you've had with bosses and peers i.e. 'How would you describe your relationship with your last boss?' They will in effect use the 'competency based rationale' even in a seemingly informal meeting. Inexperienced buyers who know they need to know it will frame the question badly i.e. 'Would you say you had a good relationship with your last boss?' This is an *extreme* closed question as it hardly invites the answer 'No I wouldn't'. But the real danger for you is that most of the buyers *don't know they need to know it* – hence the old saying in sales 'some people don't know they need something until you start selling it to them.' Well, to be more precise they do know they need to know this but only on a superficial level - not to the extent that they've really dedicated time to this beforehand and considered the questions that need to be asked and how to frame them. It's therefore incumbent on you to help them and, through your preparation, devise ways of selling critical information like this.

Take the high ground by having this conversation with yourself before turning up for the meeting: "When I leave that meeting what do I want them to know about me? Well, I want them to know I'm going to fit in and I'm a good person to have around – ok, how can I sell that, how can I weave it in, because they might not go there?" It's well worth devoting time to the above question - write out a list of the things you want to leave on the table when you're walking down the road after the meeting. I'll wager it will be more comprehensive than their shopping list.

In Plan D above, the example given to defend the 'weakness' question was of previously poor presentation skills and how the boss helped '…"but I had to get on with it and was really lucky because my boss was great at giving presentations and she gave me a lot of help…" In saying this, your body language would be sending the visual signal 'We got on really well, so we'll get on well too.' Saying you were 'really lucky' also weaves in some humility and self-deprecation – both selling points, and a way to avoid 'over-selling'. There is nothing overt about weaving the tapestry – it's a subliminal sell, sometimes conveyed by non-verbal signals.

However, making the point to the buyer that you are going to fit in is so critical that selling it subliminally i.e. 'weaving it in' may be too subtle for some buyers, so be fearless about selling it *overtly* e.g. "One of the things I've always been proud of is that wherever I've worked people have been happy to have me around". There's nothing subtle about that.

The message I want to reinforce here is that you can prepare as much as you like for these meetings, and be 'in the zone', but you are still entirely dependant on the buyer asking you the right questions, and in the right way, that will give you the opportunities to sell what you're turning up to sell. Only 2 out of 10 will do so and, as we've seen, it's within your gift to help the others.

Where do you see yourself in five years? [+]

It is pretty much understood these days by most buyers that because change is so constant and unremitting it's tricky for us to plan ahead five weeks, which might account for its decline in use. But you may still get it if the buyer has picked up an old textbook on 'How To Interview' at the last minute. It's a question that hides agendas of which they may be unaware, but which you need to consider:

1. How ambitious are you?

2. Do you have any vision?

3. Do you still see yourself with us?

4. Is your objective compatible with our plans for you (if any)?

5. If it's compatible, is it feasible within five years?

Even if you've a clear vision of what you want to be doing in five years time it's rarely a good idea to express it, except perhaps in the broadest terms, mainly because of the dangers lurking in 4 and 5 above. If the buyers can't satisfy your stated objective you've given them a reason not to hire you. The way forward is to address the underlying agenda's, send all the right signals and stay 'on side'. A sensible and helpful response might be:

"It's tricky for any of us to plan ahead these days but I try to do so (2). I do like to progress (1) and would certainly still see myself with your company (3). At this stage I've an open mind (this makes 4 and 5 redundant). My goal will be to achieve what you want me to achieve in this role, maybe more (selling added value and bringing them back to the matter at hand). Once I've done that we'll be in a better position to discuss how else I might contribute. Your business can change a lot in five years."

Do resist the temptation to respond to this question with the hackneyed: "sitting in your chair". This used to be mildly amusing in the 'womb to tomb' era and out of courtesy they will, even today, still crack a smile, but rest assured, for you the contest is over. In today's market the buyers' over-riding objective is to keep their job – not give you one. As I write, world economies are fragile and fear stalks the streets. All those you meet are in fear of losing their jobs. They won't send you those signals – but they are. It may also be your plan to cease working entirely in three years time, but keep that to yourself otherwise you send the signal that you may not be wholly committed to the task, which of course you may not, or that you are just looking for an easy ride, which you may well be. This is where you may come into conflict with Building Block 5, but a conflict easily resolved if you really do keep an open mind about where you want to be in the future.

What is your greatest achievement? [+]

Select one only. The underlying agendas are: 'What personal qualities, attributes, skills, or knowledge did you need to achieve it and do we want to buy them?' and 'How difficult was it?' There's no gain in giving an example of something that was easily achievable so try to 'weave in' the degree of difficulty, and don't go too far back in time to find your example. It's unfair but if you do so the implication is that you haven't achieved anything since. Achieving something against all the odds, *however long ago*, will be well received, as it will probably sell qualities they are seeking. The more relevant to the buyers needs the better and the more interesting the story the more time will be spent on this most excellent 'why should I hire you?' question. You want supplementary [+] questions about this that 2 out of 10 buyers will ask but 8 out of 10 won't, so you may need to follow through by telling them what it took to achieve it.

Here's an extreme example: Someone's greatest achievement may have been climbing Mount Everest 25 years ago. As a buyer meeting that same person 25 years down the line, I don't need them to climb a mountain, at least not literally. But if I know *what it takes* to climb a mountain and I'm seeking someone with strength of character, someone who can plan and organise, be tenacious, determined and resourceful; a good team player with sound judgment and good communication skills, well I'd want to hear about that achievement and I could see the relevance for myself. But if I do not have the time, experience or even intelligence to know what it takes to climb a mountain then I would need them to paint that picture for me.

What was your biggest mistake? [-]

If you're kicking leaves in the twilight zone and had no conversations with yourself before turning up then you may as well say "Coming to this meeting". That way you at least exit with a laugh and a touch of chutzpah.

You haven't come to talk about mistakes but here you are being invited to do just that. Why? What are the hidden agendas?

1. Are you honest and objective enough to recognise and admit to a mistake? If so, you're human and I might want to hire you.

2. Was it a mistake you could have avoided?

3. Do you lack sound judgment?

4. What did you learn from it?

5. What would you have done differently?

On balance we're more forgiving of mistakes made in the innocence of youth than those made later in life. So, to find that safe haven go as far back in time for your example as you feel you can legitimately go. It implies (illogically but this time to your advantage) that you haven't made any mistakes since, or at least no mistakes that big. You can also interpret the word 'mistake' as liberally as you wish, perhaps *reframe the question* (page 67) as more of a 'regret'. Trawl the waters of your education and you'll most certainly be able to haul up something that won't frighten them to death. So, after a brief pause:

"Well, hindsight is 20/20 vision (true enough) but if I had my time over again I would have:

Taken a year off before going up to University

Not taken a year off before going up to University

Stayed on at school longer but I had to get out and earn a living

Studied economics instead of mathematics."

There's bound to be something you would have done sooner, later, differently or not at all.

Alternatively, this might be where humour has a role to play. You may have an side-splitting story to tell about a big mistake you made in your first job, which at the time may have had major repercussions for your employer, but if the work/industry was completely unrelated to that being discussed, which, given the enormity of your mistake is most likely to be the case, and provided it was long ago, then only a curmudgeon would baulk at it. Fail to prepare for this and you'll most likely tell a lie and come up with something recent and relevant, not because it *is* your biggest mistake but because it is easier to recall.

With every question don't simply think through your response and leave it at that. Have more conversations e.g. 'is that a truthful response?', ' do I feel comfortable with it?', 'is it credible?' And not least 'what supplementary questions might they ask and how would I respond to those?'

What problems were there in your last role? [+]

Given that we're hired to solve problems, or stop them arising (Building Block 1) do take your time dealing with this one, making your example(s) as recent as possible. Of course it may well be that your last role is not that relevant to the one being discussed, in which case have the confidence to reframe the question: " Well, the more relevant and challenging problems arose in the role before that, where for example...." If you persist in thinking you are there to be interrogated (Building Block 2) you may not have the confidence to do any reframing.

Steer clear of any problems to do with people or personalities. If your biggest problem was your line manager you could inadvertently open a large can of worms.

Hidden agendas;

Did you cause the problem?

Could it have been avoided?

How did you solve it?

What did you learn from it?

With those last two good 'open' questions you might want to employ that structured STAR principle i.e. describe the **S**ituation, the **T**ask in hand, the **A**ction you took (this is the part you should spend most time on) and tell them the **R**esult.

It's usually safer to give an example of a problem caused by an external party, e.g. customer, client, contractor, supplier. Apportion blame lightly. It'll be a problem that couldn't have been anticipated or forestalled by you.

If you were instrumental in overcoming the problem describe, in vivid colours, what it took to do so. Take credit where credit is due, particularly with regard to decision making. Many sellers, typically the modest types, use the 'we' word too frequently which isn't helpful to buyers – at the end of the meeting it can be impossible to distinguish between what the seller achieved and what the organisation achieved. If you mean 'I decided' then say so. Yet strike the right balance because 'we' can be a good word as it can sell teamwork and the collegiate approach to decision making. And be prepared to give credit to others. As we'll see later, humility can have a role to play at these meetings. But be in no doubt – it's the 'I' word that sells you.

Are you having discussions with other organisations? [-]

Or, 'Are other buyers showing an interest in what you have to sell - if not, why am I seeing you?' All the advantages lie in you suggesting 'you bet I am'. When you convince the buyer to hire you then at some point you'll be discussing the price. One thing that gives you leverage to negotiate the price is that other buyers are talking to you. Indicating otherwise is displaying vulnerability. This is a typical 'Dead Zone 2' (page 226) question and can catch you off your guard. It'll be dressed up differently as in 'How's the job search going?' If you've allowed your 'social hat' to slip onto your head you might find yourself saying "Wow, there's blood on the streets out there – a lot of people chasing too few jobs." That's bad news (page 112).

There's an inherent balance of power at these meetings, and by its very nature it is weighted on the side of the buyer - they do, after all, 'have the cheese' (page144) and you are on their territory. This is a subliminal, not overt, 'dynamic' between buyer and seller; buyers are not sitting there thinking 'whose got the power here?' But in practice it doesn't much matter who *has* the power. If you're presenting as a 'job beggar' then they will intuitively feel *they* have the power, which they do. But, if you hold a poor hand and are *still* able to come across as a 'problem solver' then they will believe *you* have it, which you will. It doesn't really matter at all who actually has it. If as a seller you are, and feel, confident and powerful then you will almost certainly transmit those signals to the buyer, without even having to think about it. But that's easy to do. One of the dark arts of 'job' hunting in general and the magic of winning at 'interview' in particular is to always present powerfully, regardless of how vulnerable you really feel. It's often done with smoke and mirrors. It can also be great fun.

There's also much mileage to be had from letting them know you're further along the track with other buyers i.e. their competitors. Don't be too heavy handed in getting this point across. A degree of caution is necessary, as they may not have reached that optimum point at which they feel they might want to hire you, but an innocent question like 'How's your job search going?' (They still refer to 'job' instead of 'business') gives you the chance to close the net a little: "So far so good, the good news is that the world hasn't stopped (that's true) - I'm getting close with a couple of others and I'm networking like hell (aren't you?) – still got to keep my foot on the gas though". This will almost certainly register – so, not only are other buyers showing an interest in what you have to sell, YOU MAY BE CLOSE TO ANOTHER OFFER. Weaving that in can make them react as if you've just plugged them into the National Grid. It can now get competitive between buyers and, though they might have been dragging their heels up until now - boy, can they get their skates on. Whole conversations can be predicted:

Are you likely to have a decision to make on the others before we've seen you again? [+]

" I could have that dilemma."

If that happens will you call me? [+]

This is a very strong 'buy' signal and it's a great way to exit 'Dead Zone 2'. In today's market place, indicating that you're not pursuing other avenues is seen as at best poor judgment and at worst negligent. Fledgling entrepreneurs who tell others that their business is going badly may as well call in the receivers. Bad news is infectious and failure becomes a self-fulfilling prophecy. From the buyers' perspective it can be really frustrating to miss out on hiring a great candidate because they have accepted another offer *that they hadn't even obliquely mentioned*

Who are you speaking with? [-]

This is rarely asked as it borders on the impertinent. On most occasions you'll be better off selling your integrity by declining to answer the question: "They haven't advertised and they wouldn't want me to divulge their names." This can have real importance if you have secured a meeting through networking or making a direct approach, aka 'the hidden market'; they may not want it to be widely known that they are recruiting and wouldn't think well of you if you were to broadcast it to others - particularly to recruitment agencies. If you sense that you have to give them *something* then the furthest you should go is to state that they are in the same line of business. There are occasions when it can help your cause to tell them. If you're being seen by another company, generally recognised as being the market leader or in other ways prestigious then it can make them sit up and want to steal you away from under their competitor's nose.

As we've alighted on the issue of integrity this is as good a place as any to give some general guidance on this. If buyers have a mind to do so they will ask many probing questions about your previous employer e.g. their strategy and how they went about their business, the answers to which, should you provide them, would be of great interest. Yet their enthusiasm for hiring you can rapidly diminish, on the basis that if you're so freely divulging confidential information about your last employer then what are you going to be saying about them further down the line? Be prepared to dig your heels in and decline to answer any questions you feel may compromise confidentiality and your integrity; you don't want the buyer to be thinking 'you should have drawn a line under this conversation ten minutes ago'.

As a rule you should be safe divulging information already in the public domain.

How does this role compare? [-]

Damned if you do, damned if you don't. Saying that this role isn't as good as the others is unhelpful to say the least. Conversely, denigrating the others diminishes your leverage. Better to sit on the fence and not allow yourself to be drawn into making a comparison, but give a response that leaves you 'on side': "At this stage I don't have enough evidence to make a sensible comparison but given our discussion so far this role compares favourably."

It's most likely that you won't have enough evidence so you should be able to say this with some conviction. There's also something about the word 'favourably' that is neither fish nor fowl. In addition, it begs the supplementary question '**In what way?'** [+]. This allows you to talk up the positives of the role being discussed but without directly comparing it with the others.

Are you ambitious? [+]

Another extreme 'closed' question only asked by poor interviewers. You'll get a lot of these. If the meeting is turning into an interrogation it will almost certainly be because a lot of closed questions are being asked and you are failing to flesh them out. The better question would be 'How ambitious are you?' [+]

We prefer to hire people who are ambitious, but it may be unclear how much scope there is for you to achieve your ambitions within the organisation, so it may be wise to tread carefully.

It seems to be part of the human condition that many 'sellers' put a limit on to their ambitions; this betrays a lack of confidence and they are left fighting a rearguard action e.g. "I'm ambitious *bu*t I don't want to be CEO". This invites the supplementary **'Why not?' [-]** (Thus neatly turning a 'Why should I hire you?' question into an 'Why shouldn't I hire you?' one) The buyer may not be at all concerned about your not aspiring to be CEO but may be intrigued as to *why* you don't. 'Why not?' is a 'What stops your clock?' question and you should be talking about what makes you tick. 'To what heights do you think you can't aspire and why not? **[-]'** is not an avenue worth exploring from the sellers point of view because it can reveal previously hidden weaknesses to the buyer.

There's no reason why you should interpret the word 'ambitious' in ladder-climbing terms. There's nothing wrong with wanting to clamber up the corporate greasy pole but we can be ambitious in other ways: " I am ambitious in the sense that I don't like to feel I'm standing still. I want to learn new things and take on new experiences. I'm always ambitious to find out more." Make sure you have evidence to support this and be prepared to volunteer it, as they may not ask for an example.

It's an oddity of these meetings that even when we are looking for someone to come in, keep their head down and have no ambitions to progress, we still don't want them to be telling us that.

If you were recruiting someone for this role what qualities would you be seeking? [+]

Do ask this question of yourself beforehand as it's a peach of a question, and one that's really inviting you to give a shopping list of relevant qualities *that by implication you possess*. It's simply a means of getting you to look at their problem objectively and it helps them to assess whether you really know what it takes. Failing to do justice to this question is a sure indicator of failure to prepare and discourtesy because you clearly haven't bothered to analyse their problem before turning up. What does it take to solve their problem?

Does it take any of the following?

Common sense, tenacity, resourcefulness, initiative, sense of humour, qualifications, skills, experience, leadership, knowledge, contacts, empathy, understanding, accuracy, tact, diplomacy, patience, confidence, short learning curve, adaptability, honesty, reliability, determination, imagination, creativity, flexibility, courage, incisiveness, decisiveness, conviction, belief, ambition, fairness, persuasiveness, authority, inspiration, style, the ability to listen and communicate, sound judgment, teamwork, character, charisma.

If it doesn't require any of these then you may want to turn up just for the practice. Should you be unprepared for this you'd most likely be able to come up with two, maybe three relevant attributes/skills etc but with careful pre-planning it's possible to double your output e.g. "There are three things I'd say are essential for this role (now say what they are). If in addition the candidate had (now give another three) I would see that as a real bonus". You, of course, have all six.

Again – it's easy to see how it won't matter if the question isn't asked.

I've had the great privilege of coaching many thousands of modest, unassuming and capable people, not much given to 'blowing their own trumpet'. It's been great fun but desperately hard work encouraging them to articulate the 'good news' about themselves. Fortunately, we invariably had plenty of time to get the job done. The buyer simply does not have that luxury. At a meeting even our 2 out of 10 capable buyers are up against it as they may have perhaps one hour to get this information from you. That's why the 8 out of 10 desperately need your help.

Do you have an aggressive management style? [-]

'Yes' or 'No'? It's generally understood that you would be most unlikely to admit to an aggressive management style, and they would be most unlikely to want someone who has. But before responding in the negative we should consider the possible hidden agendas:

The last person in the role was too aggressive with people - we don't want another one; or the last person wasn't aggressive enough - we don't want another one.

Opt for one or the other and you've only a fifty per cent chance of getting it right - *and those odds don't get people hired*. There's a possible third hidden agenda:

Your potential boss is aggressive and this can be an oblique way of teasing out how you react to people with this management style. If you get up on your high horse and start railing against aggressive managers then you may win the battle but lose the war. You may take the view 'well, I can't work with an aggressive manager so what's the point in carrying on with the meeting - that can be someone else's problem' then you've forgotten Building Block 3. If you're going for a management role expect your management style to be dissected and be prepared to discuss it. For the buyers it is dispiriting to raise the issue of 'management style' only to be met with a blank look. Good managers should know how they get results through others. It's often not so much a question of whether there is a 'right' or 'wrong' style but more an expectation on their part that you are capable of having a meaningful discussion about it. Have the confidence to 'question the question' (page 69):

"I feel I'm adaptable enough as a manager to change my style depending on the situation and maybe the person I'm managing. People respond differently. Some only react positively to a more *assertive* style but others require a more subtle approach. Good managers should know what makes their staff tick and be able to adapt accordingly." Note also the re-framing by substituting 'aggressive' with 'assertive' - a less emotive word.

This should get the discussion off to a good start, but again, remember the importance of examples to back up what you're selling, and perhaps volunteer them as an integral part of your response.

---------♦ ♦ ♦---------

Who's Got The Cheese? A Cautionary Tale

There are certain subjects on which people can hold strong views and 'management' is one of them. When contentious issues are raised in these meetings you must express your views carefully lest positions become entrenched and subsequently polarised. Stories are legion of sellers arguing vigorously with buyers over a certain point of issue, winning the argument and leaving the meeting having won the battle but lost the war. Put your case with conviction and passion but know when to use tact and diplomacy - determination to win an argument can deflect you from your objective, which is to win the offer.

There is the story of the pompous diner who aggressively demanded that cheese be provided as a supplement to the meal. The Head Waiter politely informed him that cheese was not usually included with that particular menu. The diner became abusive and decided to pull rank. 'Do you know who I am'? 'No sir' replied the Head Waiter calmly, whereupon the diner proceeded to inform the waiter that he was a high ranking personage, one of the great and the good and a veritable mover and shaker in the world of big business - 'So cheese - NOW!' The Head Waiter quietly replied 'Do you know who I am sir'? 'No' replied the florid faced diner 'Who are you'? 'I'm the one who's got the cheese sir'.

There is a certain, indefinable 'dynamic' between buyer and seller, which can sometimes be balanced on a knife-edge, e.g. the buyer may ask a seemingly crass question, the answer to which is plain to see on your CV. Any body language from you that is screaming out 'If you'd read my CV you'd know, you dummy' will upset that dynamic - to your cost. Your CV has only been given the benefit of the doubt – to the buyer it could be the greatest work of fiction since Harry Potter – expect it to be tested for credibility and honesty. A sales meeting is a two-way process, so fight your corner firmly and politely - you'll be respected for it. But there are ways of getting what you want so remember who's got the cheese and don't drive a wedge between you and the buyer.

Do you prefer working on your own or in a team? [-]

One of those questions, because of the way it's framed, that applies pressure to choose between two or more options. Such questions are often based on a false premise so pause and consider if this is so. With this example there's no logical reason why you should have a preference. As we saw earlier (page 69) if you are thinking 'what's the right answer?' you would no doubt make your best guess and tell a lie.

If you assume that the buyer is seeking a 'team player' you might go for that option, but the way in which you express it may force the buyer to conclude that you are unable or uncomfortable when working in a role with a high degree of autonomy - which might be the very role they had in mind, if not now then further down the track. It may be that their problem requires teamwork, in which case 'a team' will be spot on (but perhaps still a lie). They may well be weighing up your potential for taking on another role, with a high degree of autonomy, maybe in a year's time, and if you indicate too strongly that working alone is not your forte they may then deduce that your potential for future development is limited, which may well be true.

To state "I don't have a preference" is fine as far as it goes but it's somewhat monochrome. Giving a straight answer to a straight question can have its virtues but too much of that and you end up with an interrogation on your hands. Better to flesh out that response by going on to give an example of when you have done both and thrived in each situation. You'll also be on safe ground stating that you see the organisation as being 'one team'.

If you could choose any job, what would it be? [-]

Such questions don't really belong within the context of a formal meeting, and they are not particularly common, yet it's one that can really throw you at an unguarded moment. This is a 'Dead Zone Two' (page 226) question if ever there was one. The 'hidden agenda' is: "this role we're discussing is not what you really want to do at all is it - so what else have you aspired to achieve?" The unprepared seller will pluck out of the ether a 'job' they have always hankered after but for one reason or another didn't acquire. More worryingly from the buyer's point of view, it may bear no resemblance to the role that the seller has spent the last hour enthusing over - no transferable skills at all. It also begs the killer supplementary 'What stopped you from achieving it?' [-].

This is another 'What stops your clock?' question. You don't want to be fighting this battle while fumbling around for your car keys. There's no mileage in giving any answer other than "This one". If the chemistry is right the buyer will be comfortable with this. If you judge that it just might come across as being too 'flip' then alternatively describe a role/task/business which is in effect the one that you have been discussing but without naming it. Giving any other example is another way of saying 'this role is second best'.

Who was your last boss? [+] [-]

This seemingly benign question no more than sets up the next one and yet the astute buyer will be watching your body language. It's nanosecond stuff and the buyer has got to be looking for it to spot it. A picture of your previous boss has now been planted in your brain. Is it a pleasant or an unpleasant picture to behold - a good relationship or not so good? A violent change of posture; an audible sigh; a scary look in the eye; a hot flush (tricky to control those - best not to think about it) and no smile are all indicators of a difficult relationship with a previous boss. A poor relationship transmits poor body language. Tellingly, a good relationship with a previous boss often elicits both a smile and a name from the seller. A poor relationship will elicit a job title, as the seller can't bear to speak the name. Throughout the meeting perceptive buyers will be looking for this congruence between verbal and non-verbal signals.

If I asked your last boss about you, what do you think he/she would tell me? [+]

Or, 'What did your previous buyer think about the product?' Such a question is designed to find out if you had a good working relationship with your boss and what kind of a person you are to work with. Did you fit in to your previous organisation (page 119)? Interestingly, "what do you *think* he/she would tell me?" impels most respondents to mirror this by saying: "I *think* she'd tell you that...". This isn't reassuring. Even worse, some respond by saying "She'd *probably* tell you....". Others really throw in the towel by saying "I *hope* she'd tell you....". The signal being sent here is 'Well, if you caught her on a good day she might say something nice about me'.

Clearly, the question is hypothetical but the most effective way to deal with it is to give an example of compliments that *were* paid, perhaps at a formal appraisal. This will allow you to conclude your response by saying ".... and if you had her here today she would repeat that." Hypothetical questions are invariably best reframed by your turning them into reality and giving real examples. Also, the buyers don't have to work so hard to get the evidence from you.

Alternatively, a good rapport with the buyer will allow you to go straight for the money and respond with a gimlet-eyed "She'd tell you to hire me." Sometimes the briefest answers have the best payoff. This is one of those questions where Building Blocks 1 - 8 all have a role to play.

What was his/her greatest weakness? [-]

Resist the temptation to say: "She was a poor judge of character" as that invalidates all the good work done in the previous question.

'Never criticise your previous boss or organisation' is one of the golden rules, and it's worth adhering to it. Yet here you are being invited to do just that. This is a 'boomerang' question, i.e. one that benignly leads you off in a safe direction but returns to unexpectedly smack you on the back of the head when you're not looking. A common response, which typifies the boomerang effect, is "Well, she wasn't good at delegating work". The buyer is now thinking that perhaps the seller was not seen to be a safe pair of hands. The frequency of this answer leads me to believe that it's pure invention - a knee jerk, on the spot response, simply because the seller is bereft of any other ideas. If it isn't then the quality of management expertise out there is sorely lacking.

Should you throw away an ill-chosen weakness it provokes the supplementary question "What did you do to help him/her overcome it?" If you did nothing but bellyache about it then here comes that boomerang.

The buyer would like to feel that the seller is at least struggling to think of a weakness so take the sting out of it and say *something* flattering about the person. "Her strengths far outweighed her weaknesses, and to think of a weakness I'd be nit-picking. But I guess she didn't really enjoy..." Now, although this is a deal breaking 'Why shouldn't I hire you?' question, with a little thought it can be turned around. This can be achieved by giving an example of a task not enjoyed by your boss, but one at which you excelled and that is relevant to the buyer's problem. This allows you to end your response by saying "...but it wasn't an issue, she recognised that as one of my strengths, was more than happy to delegate it to me and I was happy to take it on. We complemented each other well in that respect."

As an aside, so many 'sellers' have, over the years, told me that their last boss was "really bad - no good with people at all". The puzzling thing is that those bad bosses never seem to turn up as 'sellers'. I've yet to meet one of them.

Has your career developed as you would have liked? [+]

It seems to be part of the human condition that when this question is asked we instinctively start thinking about those times when things haven't gone well, and express this by saying "Yes, apart from my time at XYZ company" Or, as one recently 'downsized' seller memorably put it "Yeah – until now." Even when better framed, as "How would you assess your career to date?" it invariably generates a less than enthusiastic response.

Now, although careers are rarely seamless this isn't the time to sound off about those times when life wasn't too peachy. As there's a tendency to blame others for our misfortunes it's also tempting to criticise, directly or indirectly, previous bosses - typically those who promised much but failed to deliver. *No one wants to hear this negativity.* Take stock of your achievements and look at your career as a whole. Are you proud of what you have achieved? If you are then say so. If you're not perhaps you should reconsider your assessment. Think about any compliments that others have paid you and look for recurring themes; if others have consistently praised you for having a particular strength/attribute/quality then they can't all be wrong. Are you a worker or a shirker? Occasional brief periods of inactivity are nothing to be ashamed of, especially in today's market place. If you have, for the most part, always been in work then in itself this is something to be proud of. Say so. The word 'proud' is unfashionable these days and not one that we're much given to using in reference to ourselves but try it for size and hopefully it will grow on you.

All achievements should be measured against the backcloth of our educational and social starting point. We largely expect graduates to achieve things. It therefore comes as no surprise. We are often more intrigued and impressed by those who have achieved the same things but without the advantage of a solid family background and good schooling - it can demonstrate character, drive, resourcefulness and the ability to work hard and get on with others - all qualities in high demand. But we know that not all buyers have the intelligence, insight or *time* to figure this out for themselves - you must 'have the conversations with yourself'. Only then will you be able to articulate them with clarity to the buyer. A good response to this question should get across all your virtues such as hard work, commitment, progress, having had good bosses/mentors, working for good organizations, tenacity – if you've got it sell it, otherwise how will they know? Deliver this good news e.g.

'I've worked really hard.'

'I've worked for some good organisations.'

'I've been lucky to have had some great mentors along the way.'

'I've never felt I was standing still.'

'I've always enjoyed what I was doing.'

'I've met some inspiring people and learned a lot from them.'

'I've always been appreciated - colleagues seemed happy to have me around.'

'I've been asked to take on some challenging roles.'

' I've always felt I was making a real contribution.'

These positives should all provoke supplementary 'Why should I hire you?' questions so think through what they might be. A word of caution: if your career has been one of rapid and continual promotion and you've worked for organisations that have met with great success don't get complacent as the buyer may not automatically assume *you* are a winner - a rising tide floats all boats.

Would you be prepared to relocate? [-]

If no previous reference to relocation had been made this question can come as a real curved ball. The immediate reaction is to start thinking of all the reasons why relocation would be impossible (partner's job, children's education etc.) and then express those fears. At best we try to be positive but put reservations on it: "It would depend on where you might relocate to". It doesn't 'depend' on anything. If you want to stay in the game there's only one sensible response: "For the right role and the right organisation I can't see that relocation would be a issue". But if you know that relocation is impossible, surely there would be no point in saying otherwise, as you would be wasting everyone's time? Perhaps, but why might the question be asked? They may be seeking to establish the depth of your long-term commitment to them, and this is one way of doing it. Interpret the question too literally and you may be travelling down the wrong road. Why not ask them straight out if they are planning to relocate? *Because right now you don't need to know – you just want them to ask you some more 'Why should I hire you?' questions.*

If you respond enthusiastically but have real reservations about it then when you get the offer a few weeks or months down the line a simple phone call can check it out. If they say that they are definitely relocating (highly unlikely as it would have been made much clearer at the meeting) then you have a decision to make. Respond negatively and you will have no call to make. Remember Building Block 3.

Beware the 'nine day wonder'. At any given time in organisations there is often an issue that, although founded on no more than rumour, becomes a major talking point. It tends to kick around for about nine days before dying a natural death. 'Relocation' is not an uncommon example of this. 'Nine day wonders' have a habit of invading these meetings and can be presented to you as fact.

Have you ever failed in any job you have tried to do? [-]

Now 'failure' is not a topic you have come to discuss, but here they are inviting you to do just that. It is not a particularly useful question as it merely invites the response "Not that I recall" which doesn't take the conversation very far, and although there is much to be said for brevity with these **[-]** questions the accompanying body language might present a problem. Failure can be another relative concept and this allows you to talk in terms of 'degrees of success'. For example: "I've never failed to achieve what's been expected of me. Over and above that I set myself higher personal targets and I can't say that I've always met those. For example..." Go on to give an example of a task you've undertaken which met a previous buyers expectations but not your own. Upping the ante in this way allows you to demonstrate that they're not talking to someone who is content to turn up and do the minimum. You, unlike your competitors, are always looking to go the extra mile and add value.

A Word About Humility

When you're selling yourself on your CV to achieve these meetings humility has little or no role to play. But during the meeting it can play an important part, as you may sometimes need to sell it.

Another important 'dynamic' of these meetings is that all buyers like to feel that they are getting somewhere. They expect to find a few chinks in your armour. If you 'over-sell' they might begin to think that you're too good to be true. This is professionally frustrating for them and thus disadvantageous for you. You must be alert to this and if you feel you are 'over-selling' you ought to take your foot off the gas. If you're waxing too lyrical about your achievements then sell some humility by giving credit to others. Throw them a bone to chew on if you perceive that they are getting hungry. But you're more likely to be in danger of underselling, otherwise why read this book? Having read this far you may still, even now, be harbouring some doubts about the necessity of selling yourself in a competitive marketplace. You may even find it in some way distasteful, in which case take succour from this: Yet another interesting 'dynamic' of these meetings is that 'buyers' can also be 'sellers' and they will, if their need is urgent and your skills rare in the market, do a pretty good job of selling the organisation/role to you. They won't go out of their way to tell you why you *shouldn't* join them. They will play up the strengths of the role and hide the 'downsides'. Or, you may have come highly recommended by a mutual network contact, which puts you in a more powerful position as the buyer may have to do a selling job on you to encourage you to join them – why would they give you reasons not to?

Moreover, if they're in the private sector they represent a company that has a product or service to sell – that company may invest huge sums of money per annum on its own PR/Sales & Marketing. So here's what you might want to do - get hold of *their* sales literature before the meeting and carefully study what they say about their product. Now find the bit where they tell you what its greatest weakness is. You might find it next to the section highlighting why you *shouldn't* buy their product. If it's not there you might stumble across it under the heading 'Pending Lawsuits'. Now turn up for that meeting and do what you have to do, it is after all a two way process, but don't portray that you are a candidate for canonisation.

If one of your team ceased to perform what would you do about it? [+]

Or, 'Are you the kind of manager we want to hire?' The ability to exercise sound judgment, tact, firm decision making, common sense, trust and compassion are all qualities that this question allows you to promote. The key to it is the word 'ceased' and it's this that most sellers fail to pick up on. It implies that the individual was previously performing well. Given that people don't stop performing without reason this should be the main thrust of your answer, i.e. you'd presumably take the person to one side, voice your concerns about the drop in performance, allow them to express their views and reach some kind of mutual agreement on what can be done about it. You may even invite other team members to offer up solutions. Your actions may need to be more robust as it might depend on the nature of the role and how the drop in performance manifests itself. If, for example, it impacted badly and immediately on customers or other members of the team then action may need to be swift. If you can think of an appropriate example of when you have been in such a situation and explain how you resolved it, so much the better. Try not to offer up a 'one size fits all' remedy to these hypothetical scenarios as you may come across as one dimensional and incapable of thinking laterally.

How do you motivate people? [+]

This is another opportunity to sell your management style. Extolling the virtues of teamwork, the ability to correctly identify the 'drivers' in each individual (e.g. most people are motivated by praise) intuition, leading by example and sound communication skills can all be brought into play here. Time for another word of caution: IF YOU HAVEN'T GOT IT - DON'T SELL IT -Building Block 5 is your anchor so only sell what you possess. Doing otherwise is wrong, unhelpful, unnecessary, and you wouldn't be able to back it up. Do your self- analysis, identify the qualities you do possess and figure out ways of getting them across, against the backcloth of your understanding of their problem. Look at your CV before the meeting. You've designed it to provoke questions – what questions are you provoking? If you're selling 'leadership' or 'motivating others' then get ready for those probing questions.

Would you accept this position if we offered it to you? [-]

An encouraging question as it can be a strong 'buy' signal. Yet it's potentially dangerous as an ill judged response can suck you into a premature discussion on remuneration, and as we'll discover later, nearly all discussions on the price are premature. This question would typically arise towards the end of the process, when the buyer has made a positive decision and is seeking to gauge your level of interest. For obvious reasons we can rule out 'No' as an appropriate response but don't be steamrollered into saying 'Yes' (if the remuneration hasn't been discussed you would find this a strange notion anyway).

It's more than likely that some things have yet to be discussed (not least the price) so you're not in possession of enough facts to make a decision, therefore a qualified 'yes' is appropriate. But be careful *how* you qualify it; "Yes, depending on terms and conditions" or the more coy " Yes, but we haven't discussed everything yet" or the crass "I can't make a decision until I have something in writing" (why not – don't you trust me?) or the thinly veiled threat "I do have other things to consider" (well, you go right ahead and consider them then while I offer it to someone else) are all snatching defeat from the jaws of victory and the discussion can get bogged down – you're close to making the sale so don't allow it to unravel now.

Better to seize the initiative and respond thus: "On the basis of what we've discussed (therefore by implication there are still things to be ironed out; now follow that with the soft 'yes') - I'm really enthusiastic".

Now close the sale by asking two questions: "How soon could you get a written offer to me?" This implies that you've inferred from their question, *and it's only in your interests to infer it*, that they're going to offer it to you - so *when* is it going to come? It also diplomatically makes the point that you can't give a definitive answer until you have it in writing, "and how soon after that would you need my response?" This is saying two things to the buyer:

1. Don't assume I'm going to bite your hand off - so think carefully about the price.

2. I may have other offers, so how much time do I have to pull it all together?

Closing the sale can elicit: 'We could get a written offer to you by Friday and we'd need your response one way or the other by next Wednesday.' At which point you should already be standing up, reaching for your hat and coat, making the right noises ('you've made my day') and getting the hell out of there. Don't carry on selling – you're that close to winning the prize.

The right chemistry between buyer and seller can allow for a bolder approach:

Would you accept this position if we offered it to you?

Are you offering it to me? (smile)

Yes

Great - well on the basis of what we've discussed I'm really enthusiastic. How soon could you get a written offer to me, and how soon after that would you need my response?

Of course there is an alternative:

Would you accept this position if we offered it to you?

Are you offering it to me? (remember to smile)

No

Difficult to gauge where the conversation might go after that, but they're either offering it to you or they're not. If they are then the above robust approach from you can encourage them to get on with it. If they're not then they really shouldn't ask silly questions. It may require great discipline for you, the seller, to stop yourself from raising the issue of remuneration – you will after all be burning up with curiosity to know the figures. And yet this is 'above the line' (Building Block 1) information *that you don't need to know now.*

A word of warning: It is a common experience for buyers to send you positive signals and strongly imply that you are going to get the offer in writing, only for you to never hear from them again. You could waste two weeks or more of your valuable time waiting for the offer that never comes - keep your foot on the gas and keep selling on all other fronts. They may also ask you, *and perhaps your one remaining competitor*, to return for 'an informal chat' with the MD, CEO or other head honcho 'just to say hello'. Don't saunter into that meeting with your 'social hat' perched at a cocky angle - they often turn out to be the most brisk and probing of all. Be prepared and you will know it is safe to enter. Let your competitor be the canary in the coalmine.

Why haven't you found a job yet? [-]

This question would only arise if the buyer were aware that you've been in the market for some time and it borders on the impertinent. The not so hidden agenda; 'Why doesn't anyone want to hire you?' **[-]** invites you to become defensive and sound off about how tough it is out there in the marketplace. The question assumes that other buyers haven't wanted to hire you. If you've received other offers but turned them down then say so. "This is a critical stage in my career and it's important I make the right decision. I've had offers which had their merits but they weren't right for me - and if it's not right for me it's not right for the organisation."

This puts you back in the driving seat and politely implies that the buyer had better not assume that you'd necessarily jump at any offer *they* might make.

It's often the case that you'll get invited to meetings that you're disinclined to attend. Always turn up for them. Why?

1. You need as much practice as you can get. If you're new to the market place it will typically take you six meetings to get up to speed. Better to hone your skills and articulate your truth at meetings that don't matter.

2. It's not unusual to find yourself discussing a role other than the one you turned up to discuss (Building Block 3). It may become apparent to the buyer very quickly that the problem being discussed won't stretch you enough and hold your interest, but if you're displaying enthusiasm for working with them they'll maybe consider you as the solution to other problems they might have - and which they haven't yet got around to advertising

and for which you have no competitors. If you don't turn up you'll never uncover these little gems.

3. You're passing up a networking opportunity. Go along with your own agenda, e.g. to find out more about their competitors, the market or their network contacts and come away with at least one other lead.

4. Get them to offer it to you so that you can turn it down. You can then go to subsequent meetings and deal with this question with honesty and conviction.

Try not to let a long job search get you down and never let others diminish you because of it. "I'm better off taking a year to get the right job than getting the wrong job in one month" is a signal of strength you can articulate at the meeting ('balance of power' page 132).

How important is money to you? [+] [-]

This question is designated [+] and [-] as it is in the 'corridor of uncertainty'. Our two out of ten experienced buyers will give much thought not only to the questions they will ask but how those questions should be framed. They will choose their words carefully and be interested in your analysis and understanding of the question. Only after your analysis and response does it become clear, if not to you then to the buyer, whether this is a [+] 'why should I hire you?' or a [-] 'why shouldn't I hire you?' question, hence the 'corridor of uncertainty'. Take your time to think about these questions as buyers want considered responses not just knee-jerk answers. Here, the buyer is not asking: "how important is *the* money to you?" which might imply they were referring to the remuneration package, but 'how important is money *as a concept*' or 'When I say the word 'money' what does it trigger in your brain – salary or profit'?

Sellers not 'in the zone' turn this into a [-] by feebly taking a swat at the salary ball. Unfortunately this isn't the ball being delivered. Compounding the error they invariably go on to eschew the importance of it: "It's important but it's not everything. Other things are more important at this stage in my career such as job satisfaction" (they now make heroic efforts to regain the high ground and not come across as a pushover) "but I do need to maintain my standard of living." This is like Buster

Keaton on ice - all over the place. With a hapless answer like that those nasty supplementary 'above the line' questions are queuing up: **'What's your present salary?'** [-] **'What salary are you looking for?'** [-] **'What do you need to maintain your standard of living?'** [-] You would be much better off indicating that money is important and no 'buts' about it – just make sure you put it in the buyers context (below the line) and see it as the **[+]** that it was intended to be all along: "Well, money is extremely important-it's the bottom line. You're in business to make a profit and we'd all do well to remember that. Not just profits but cost effectiveness, budgetary constraints - value for money is also important. If we stay focused on that the company will stay successful and everyone in it will be happy." (NOW HIRE ME!)

Or, just in case you're discussing a problem in the 'Not For Profit' Sector: "Money is really important - we're spending taxpayer's money/charitable donations and we're accountable to them. We have a duty of care and must be mindful of this."

This allows you to say that money is important but because the vehicle you're using to get the point across is *their* money (below the line [+]) and not yours (above the line [-]), you won't get bogged down in a premature discussion on the price. It also implies that you won't be a pushover when it does come to discussing it. If ever a question were designed to find out which type of seller you are (Building Block 1) this is it. Now, it's unlikely, but if the buyer delivered the supplementary: " That's great but I was really talking about the salary" then you could truthfully say " Well, in effect so was I but my argument is that we can't expect decent salaries (above the line) if we don't care about making a profit (below the line) - the one comes before the other."

In Building Block 4 we saw that there's a strong element of role-playing at these meetings. But it's a two-way process so buyers role-play too! With our 'social' hat on our head we can all appreciate that there are more important things in life and money certainly isn't the 'be all and end all'. But with our 'buyer' hat on we sure don't want to hear any of that nonsense.

Because our brains are all wired up differently, words and their context can be interpreted and understood in myriad ways; if they are seeking someone who is innately entrepreneurial then the word 'money' for such people triggers the word 'profit' and not 'salary'- it just registers on a different scale. The message here is that with preparation your 'colour' can have a more attractive hue.

If you are attempting to make a career transition *from* the 'not for profit' sector to the private sector this may be their method of assessing your awareness of, and enthusiasm for, the profit imperative. For sure, if their need is for you to have finely honed financial skills/awareness e.g. finance director, accountant, negotiator, buyer (!) then you'd better not make a hash of this one.

You do not have all the experience we are seeking [-]

Or, ' Because you don't have this experience I can't hire you can I?' Here, an aspect of the role is being highlighted of which you have no previous experience or perhaps knowledge. The buyer needs some strong reassurance from you that this won't be an issue.

Building Block 7 tells us that if you get the meeting the buyer must consider that, at the very least, you could *possibly* be the solution to their problem. Indeed, it's typically this 'objection' that makes you a 'possible' as opposed to a 'probable'. Logic tells us then that this 'objection' cannot be insurmountable otherwise why would they call the meeting? Yet you don't surmount it simply by saying 'I don't think that'll be a problem.'

This is easier to defend if you've done your homework and asked yourself the 'Why might they *not* hire me?' question. When buyers put an objection on the table, which they know could easily have been anticipated, their enthusiasm wanes when the seller looks mystified - the body language clearly displays lack of preparation and forethought.

With preparation you can really blow them out of the water by giving a hatful of reasons why it won't be a problem:

1. You are confident. Selling 'confidence' is helpful but you must be coming across as confident. To avoid 'over selling' you may feel the need to take the sting out of this by adding "…not over-confident – I wouldn't be complacent about it".

2. You have common sense. Everyone wants to buy that but may not realise it until you sell it.

3. You have a short learning curve. Again, to avoid over selling you might be wise to add "…. I can't promise I can hit the ground running on this but…"

4. You can give an example (and we know how important they are) of a role you took on in the past, with limited experience, and succeeded - a precedent has been set. If it wasn't a problem then, why should it be a problem now? Tell them the story and provide some evidence. Another example of how the 'competency based rationale' can work for you even in a non-competency based 'interview'.

5. Persuade them to see it as an advantage. It's not generally recognised in recruitment, although it should be, that it's not always advantageous to hire someone with all the experience as it presents

retention issues i.e. that the role might not stretch them and they won't stick around for long. They may also be too set in their ways. Because this is not generally understood it's only when you reveal this to the buyer that they see the wisdom of it, and the logic of this sound argument could scare the daylights out of them and eliminate your more experienced competitor.

6. Explain you can offer them 90% of the experience they do need - if you had 100% you wouldn't be at the meeting. In reality this is the good old 80/20 rule. You should be seeking the *right* problem to solve and that shouldn't be a role for which you have all the experience. If you have everything then you'll have nothing new to add to your CV for the *next time* you're in the market (a gloomy thought but the 'shelf-life' of jobs these days is pretty limited).

It's not enough to present the buyer with just one of the above as this won't be enough ammunition to give them the confidence to fight the battle on your behalf. So, it's simply a matter of formulating a response which includes as many of the above as you can support. A heartening preamble to your response is: " I've given this a lot of thought and it won't be an issue for many reasons...." Now the buyer is already reassured because you've clearly anticipated it. Also, you're now going to give a whole shopping list of reasons - this will have them salivating on the edge of their seats, and structure your response by using that competency based rationale that previous performance\behaviour is a fairly strong predictor of how you would perform in the future:

"Firstly, when I took on my previous role (**S**ituation) I had no experience of ----- (**T**ask). But with a combination of common sense, confidence and a short learning curve (**A**ctions you took, and spend more time painting this part of the picture) I came out of it well (**R**esult) - I've done it before so I can do it again. Also it could even be a huge advantage; you could offer this to someone who's done it all before but they might get easily bored and walk away a month down the line. They might also be blinkered in their approach - I can come at it with a fresh mind, give it my own imprint and maybe do it better than them. Finally, I've a good 90% of the experience you do need; if I had 100% we wouldn't be talking. It's my intention to broaden my experience and by definition that means taking on something new".

Yes - that last one is 'above the line' but legitimate on this occasion.

Again, remember there are different ways of articulating the same points. For example, 6 above could be expressed by saying " That's why we call it career development – I've never taken on a role for which I have all the experience because you don't learn anything new." Or, for those of you who have been buyers, 5 above could be expressed by "I've never offered a role to anyone who has all the experience because they tend to be blinkered in their approach and don't stick around if it doesn't stretch them. That's a false economy."

Although most of the meetings you attend may not be structured 'competency based interviews' as such, I strongly advise that as the seller you use the competency based rationale at any meeting you attend and it isn't complicated; it's simply a means of ensuring that you turn up with real evidence, based on past experience. Far too many 'sellers', when asked for an example, don't give one at all - they just talk in generalities. This is very frustrating for the buyer.

This 'objection' is the exception to the rule that brevity is wise for **[-]** questions - see 'Don't Shoot The Messenger.'

Don't Shoot The Messenger

When an objection to hiring you is put on the table do not assume that the person raising it is the one who actually sees it as an issue. The way they frame the objection may suggest they do see it as an issue as they would most likely 'take ownership' of it e.g. "I see you as a strong candidate (that's a clue that they are ok with it) but one concern *I* have is your lack of experience in this sector".

To secure the offer you're likely to be attending more than one meeting. The one with the 'cheese' may not come into the frame until the final meeting. At the first meeting your objective is to get to the next one. Dangers lurk when buyers disagree on what they are looking for. HR managers and recruitment firms, who may be conducting the first meeting, are 'gatekeepers' and they can disagree strongly with line-managers/clients about what it takes to solve the problem i.e. the skills, knowledge, attributes, experiences or qualifications required for the role. If the one with the cheese has an objection recognised *but not necessarily shared* by the 'gatekeeper' managing the first meeting, that person is almost certain to raise it as a 'cry for help'. Failure to understand this can result in you displaying negative body language ('What the hell am I doing here then?') or fighting a battle over the issue and leaving the first meeting without having given the buyer any ammunition to fire. That first buyer (who has seen your CV and decided to meet you) is your ambassador and will be expected to make a case for you in any subsequent discussion with the decision maker, who may be unaware of your existence when the first meeting is taking place, - and a discussion in which you are rarely a participant.

The 'gatekeeper' may have to sell you convincingly to the one who has the power to hire you and that's why you must give as comprehensive a defence as you can to the apparent objection 'You do not have all the experience we are seeking'. The credibility of a gatekeeper is always on the line so if you cannot give a robust defence to them they are not inspired to promote your case to others.

Remember-if you've got the meeting it's yours to lose – (Building Block 7).

---------♦ ♦ ♦---------

Don't you think you're over–qualified / too experienced? [-]

This is more frustrating than being accused of not having enough experience. Hidden agenda's;

1. It won't stretch you; you'll get bored and won't stick around.

2. You won't fit in.

3. You're a threat.

4. You may be too expensive.

5. You're looking for a soft option where you can freewheel.

It can of course also be a euphemism for 'You're too old'.

Before turning up do seriously consider if any of 1-5 apply. You will still attend the meeting (Building Block 3) but the dangers of 'under–selling' yourself are very real. As we have seen, the right role is the one for which you don't have all the experience/knowledge, not one for which you have too much. You are only as good as your last job and your last salary, so if you are even the slightest bit interested in developing your career then surely your CV should be growing, not standing still or going backwards? Here's another paradox - it's not as easy as you might think to persuade a buyer to let you solve a problem beneath your capability, and price. Doctors don't like their nurses to be too intelligent and they may well think you won't stick around or may even present a threat to them.

The best you can do with this is to express mild surprise (a raise of the eyebrows should suffice) and defend thus; "I don't believe so. A job is what you make it and I give total commitment to whatever I do. I may have more experience than you need right now but it may be added value for the future as your business grows. Also I would be a good mentor for the team."

Best to steer clear of defending 4 above as it could suck you into a premature discussion on the price; unless you already know what their price is, in which case you may as well throw in "You'd be getting great value for money."

It's also not improbable that the buyer is planning to move on in the near future and is, perhaps covertly, seeking a successor, in which case the 'objection' may not be as strong as it appears.

What can you offer us? [+]

If 'Tell me about yourself' hadn't previously come up then this is where your preparation for it comes in useful.

There's no advantage in offering things they won't want to buy so be specific and talk about relevant issues. Avoid repetition - if you haven't done your homework the pictures you paint will have no depth. This question is not easy to deal with if the meeting has arisen from a direct or networking approach because their needs may not be clearly defined and explained. In such situations offer them things that any organisation would want to buy, regardless of the role, and invite them to talk about their problem:

" In general I can offer you enthusiasm, 100% commitment, the ability to get on with people and plenty of initiative. To be more specific I'd need to know more about your needs. How clearly are these defined in your mind?"

What would you expect to achieve in your first 100 days? [+]

Any body language from you that conveys the signal 'beats me' will send them into the arms of Morpheus. This is no time for pausing and chin stroking. This is the opportunity to demonstrate that you are an expert in your field and that you understand, with clarity, the extent of their problem, what needs to be done and how it should be done. What is your thinking and methodology? Can you see the 'big picture'? Have conversations with yourself about budgetary constraints, building relationships, resources and priorities.

There is much colour to be applied here if you can build your picture by drawing on previous relevant experience. It may sometimes be politic for you to temper your enthusiasm for getting things done; for example, if there are two or more buyers in the meeting who appear to hold conflicting views you may have to perform a balancing act to keep them all 'onside'. There may be an unspoken fear that you are one of those people that come in on day one and start changing everything before consulting anyone, thus alienating others, creating general mayhem and departing in six weeks leaving scorched earth in your wake. Conversely, there may be some 'quick fixes' to implement just to let people know you've arrived.

You may even have to rein them in a little if you feel they are being unrealistic about what can be achieved in a given time frame. Don't be so keen to impress that you become the gift that keeps on giving e.g. you may be asked to give a short presentation on how you would 'solve the problem'. Leave them in no doubt that you know your stuff, and you may be able to demonstrate that their problem is more serious than even they believed it to be, but don't be overly generous with your proposed solutions.

Do you ever have doubts about your ability to do a job? [-]

Logic tells us that an enthusiastic 'Yes - frequently' would not be advisable. It thus invites the knee-jerk response 'No, not really' which might suggest that you're too confident by half. Although taking on the right role shouldn't provoke a crisis of confidence it should stretch your abilities to the full. If only to avoid that complacency it's quite healthy to feel an element of self doubt. If you think back over previous tasks you have undertaken there may be one which really did stretch you and which may have caused you some anxiety at the start. If you came out of it well and achieved the objectives - (perhaps by staying calm under pressure and having a good team around you) this could be an excellent example to give:

"Not on a day-to-day basis, but when I take on new tasks I like to feel that they'll present me with real challenges. For example...." If you can construct your response by *ending* with "...but when I take on new tasks I like to feel that they'll present me with real challenges." you stand a high chance of provoking the supplementary question 'Given your understanding of this role, what challenges will it present'? [+]

If the interests of your boss and your staff conflicted, with whom would you side? [-]

This is a test of your management and conflict resolution skills, your speed and independence of thought and not least your common sense. It's also another one of those questions seemingly forcing you to choose one of two options. The less confident seller would instinctively respond with "I'd always side with the boss". That may be unwise. The sensible route to take would surely be one that indicated your actions would depend upon the particular nature of the issue: "It would depend on the nature of the conflict. If I felt my boss was right I'd see it as my responsibility to communicate that clearly to my staff. On the other hand, if I believed my staff had a valid grievance I would seek to resolve this sensibly with my boss." You could also point out that you wouldn't see it as 'taking sides': "Everyone in the business should be pulling in the same direction so we're all on the same side". A good response should display that 'you are your own person' and can make your own decisions. Giving an example of when you were in such a situation would obviously strengthen your response, but you can't always do that so you may have to keep it hypothetical.

What was your previous salary? [-]

It takes much confidence and preparation to deal with this effectively. But remember - preparation builds confidence. The policy of giving a straight answer to a straight question can have much to commend it, but not necessarily in this case. In the old days when we were 'applying for jobs' and being hired on a so-called 'permanent' basis this was seen as a legitimate question. Even then a few more enlightened buyers understood how impertinent it was and rightly declined to ask it. It's never been a legitimate question in the wider world of business, and now that we are all 'business people' it has even less credence. If we slightly re-phrase the question as 'How much did your previous buyer/customer pay for your services?' we can see how impertinent it is.

Does the buyer or seller open at a price? Well, whoever opens is potentially in the weaker bargaining position. In my experience sellers who give a straight answer i.e. divulge their previous remuneration, get offered (if they get hired at all) either exactly the same, or a bit more or a bit less. As the seller you may feel that this would still be a satisfactory result, and it may, but you are likely to discover, some months later, and too late, that your colleagues are being paid more for undertaking the same work, and in a free market your grounds for complaint are flimsy.

Alternatively, if you feel that your previous remuneration was 'high' compared to your perception of what the market will bear, and you divulge it, the buyer's enthusiasm for continuing the discussion may diminish because they can't afford you. Try convincing them that you would be content to take a cut in remuneration and they may nod sagely but it's falling on deaf ears. Also, carrying the burden of a high previous price tag may impel you to make an impulsive and voluntary concession which might have proved unnecessary " My previous salary was £xx plus xxx - but I don't need to match that at this stage in my career." - Whoops! For these reasons the question is of crucial significance.

Have a defensive strategy in place that is well considered and rehearsed. Whether you adopt it in practice will depend on both the timing and your judgment on the buyers attitude, demeanour and, perhaps not least, sense of humour. Giving the straight answer is potentially disadvantageous but it is not failure. Trying to evade the question with uncooperative buyers will inevitably lead to a breakdown in communications and even confrontation, in which case you lose because they have the cheese.

Should the question come in the early stages of the meeting then the real problem is not so much that they've asked the question but that they've asked it too soon. The obvious remedy then is to invite them to come back to it later. Now this can be achieved with a simple 'Can we come back to this later?' but the chances are not high with the more assertive buyer. As an alternative you could try something more structured e.g. "Let's talk about the overall package as salaries can be misleading..." this makes a useful distinction because if you are going to discuss it now, better to be talking about the big picture. Next, and pause for breath here (you're going to need it and they won't interrupt) –"but perhaps we can come back to this later?" This implies that you will be happy to answer the question later, which of course you may, and it also implies 'later on in this meeting' whereas it could mean a subsequent meeting - a useful ambiguity. Don't pause for breath now though because the assertive buyer will interject - don't give them the chance) "it might be more helpful at this early stage if I find out more about the role and you find out more about me and what I can bring to it."

This tempts the buyer, and certainly the more assertive buyer, to ask the supplementary: "Sure, we can come back to it - what *can* you bring to it?" [+] The buyer is now saying 'Why should I hire you? [+]' as opposed to 'How much are you going to cost me?' [-]

Some buyers will still dig their heels in, suggesting they don't want to waste your time by going through the whole process only to discover late in the day that they can't afford you.

This is your opportunity to seize the initiative and invite them to open e.g. "If that should happen I won't feel I've wasted my time.... ('It's not my problem ') but I don't want to waste your time...('so as it's *your* problem')... what package do you have in mind?" ('Let's solve *your* problem working from *your* price, not mine'). The buyer now has no other option but to open or back off. In cold print this may appear too assertive for your tastes and during the dialogue you may feel more than a little tense, but with the right body language, including a smile, you can quite easily deflect the question.

Maintain your insouciance if the buyer opens at a price and don't stick your nose into the trough. Letting your curiosity get the better of you by asking questions about their figures and you could lose the prize - there comes a point when it's too late to say you'd rather discuss it later on, and you reach that point as soon as you start discussing it. *Don't discuss the price until you've made the sale.*

Should the buyer open at a price higher than your previous remuneration you'll be mighty pleased you didn't open but remain inscrutable. If they open at a level below your expectations you may be tempted to reach for your hat and coat and make for the exit, but resist and maintain that inscrutability. Unless their figure is so low and it's a dead cert you'll never be able to negotiate up to your needs then stick with it. The early stages are fertile ground for misunderstanding, miscommunication and confusion (Building Block 3). When figures are bandied around during these meetings they can bear little relation to the figures that appear in the written offer weeks later - for better or worse.

What salary are you seeking? [-]

Oh my. Now there's nothing impertinent about this question. It's entirely legitimate for the buyer to request some indication regarding the likely cost of your services, just as it is in any other business. Yet it presents the same problem in that you're still being asked to open at a price. Given that one of your objectives at the meeting is to find out more about the work needing to be done, and one of their objectives is to assess your ability to do it, there's little point in discussing the price, and how can you cost out if you don't have all the facts? Although we can understand the buyer's curiosity and impatience in wanting to know, the best course of action is to treat it in the same way as the previous question:

"I've an open mind. I'd rather talk about the package, as salaries can be misleading (pause) But maybe we can come back to this later (no pause) it might be more helpful at this early stage if I find out more about the role and you find out more about me and what I have to offer?"

If the 'chemistry' isn't right give a straight answer but think it through carefully before turning up. At what level are you going to pitch your price? Give a figure which is too low in their eyes and they may feel you do not value your own services. Their enthusiasm for taking the meeting further will dim because you are obviously not 'heavy-weight' enough for the role. Giving a figure that is just about acceptable to you and more than acceptable to them will typically elicit the response 'Well that won't be a problem'; leaving you wondering what else you might have achieved if only you'd had the courage and confidence to pitch it higher.

Have three levels of remuneration in mind:

1. Your 'bottom line'. This is the level of remuneration below which you're not prepared to go. Where you pitch it is up to you. It may be your previous/present level of remuneration. It may represent a level below that i.e. the bare minimum on which you can survive/maintain your existing standard of living. This can of course *be* your existing or previous remuneration.

Vulnerable sellers will often make a huge impulsive and unnecessary concession by opening at their bottom line: "Well, the *least* I could accept is...." Now that's exactly what they will get, if they get anything at all. Impertinent buyers will *ask* for your bottom line; "What is the lowest salary you would be prepared to work for?"

2. Your 'settlement price'. This is the level of remuneration, above your bottom line, at which you would be happy to reach agreement. It will be, in your judgment, a fair and equitable price for the work they want you to do (and remember - you may at this stage lack clarity on this). You may wish to pitch it at your present level of remuneration but it should, ideally, be above that. On the other hand, if you are changing career or location then your previous remuneration may have no bearing on the issue.

3. Your 'opening price'. This is the level, above your settlement price, at which you'll open should you decide to do so. Where do you peg this? Firstly, it must be above your settlement price, as *you never open at the price at which you would be prepared to settle*. The danger is that you could still put an opening price on the table that is below what the buyer is willing and able to pay. Given that it's easier for the seller to negotiate down than up you may as well go for it and open at a price to take their breath away. In so doing you can 'fly a kite' and flush the buyer out and into revealing their top price, if only to avoid further embarrassment:

"That's a lot higher than we anticipated. I don't think we could agree on that."

Now seize the opportunity:

"Well what figure do *you* have in mind?"

"Well, the *most* we could go to is...."

Now hopefully their 'most' is somewhere between your opening price and your settlement price. You can now reel the kite in and make conciliatory noises by suggesting that your figure was maybe a little on the high side and say you remain interested in continuing the discussion. Before volunteering your opening price you may choose to throw in a caveat or two to take the sting out of it. Useful caveats are:

"I don't want to undersell or oversell myself."

"I've an open mind"

"The right role for me would not be based solely on the remuneration – I would look at it in the round."

They may respond to your opening price by saying:

" Are you worth that much?" This might encourage you to go on the defensive: "Well, I'm sure we could reach a mutually acceptable package below that." Resist this and respond more robustly: "I believe I'm worth *more* than that but I've got to be realistic."

We are of course only worth what someone is prepared to pay but on the whole we get more respect by putting a high price on our talents.

Another alternative is to 'play the green card' i.e. "Well I haven't been in the market for long and don't have a handle on the market rate – I was hoping you could maybe give me a steer on that – what package are you thinking of offering?" This is the only time it pays to be seemingly unprepared.

Buyers may prefer to choose 'What salary are you looking for?' as their 'Columbo Question' (page 226).

* This is a big topic and is covered in much greater depth in 'How To Negotiate Your Salary'.

The End Game

Most buyers will allocate some time at the end of the meeting to deal with any questions you want to ask. This 'End Game' is crucial, as 'exits' are just as important as 'entrances'. Most sellers play an inadequate End Game and leave the buyer with a poor impression, often undoing all the good work they've done in the preceding discussion. Imagine that the buyer has specifically allocated fifteen or more minutes to deal with your questions:

Are there any questions you would like to ask me? [+]

"No, you've answered all my questions, so I don't have any at this stage."

"Right - well, thanks for coming and I wish you every success in your next role - wherever that may be."

What a comedy of errors. That stage is now leaving and you are on it. *You're out of the game.* The buyer is left with no option but to terminate the meeting early, your performance ends on a low note and the last impression, which is as important as the first impression, is that the seller had no meaningful questions to ask and is thus disinterested in the role. It also sets up a less than scintillating 'Dead Zone Two'.

From bitter experience we have come to almost expect sellers to end in this way. Instead of seeing this as an opportunity to carry on selling themselves they see it as an opportunity to get their coat on and get out fast. Your exit must be memorable, but for all the right reasons.

Having no questions to pose at the end is a sure sign of having arrived at the meeting with too few. Turning up with two or three is not enough because they'll be the very ones that will be answered during the meeting.

Insure against this by preparing a list of perhaps a dozen questions that you might reasonably ask - if some are dealt with during the discussion the remainder will still allow you to play a solid 'End Game'. If none of them are closed off during the meeting then you can choose those you prefer to ask.

If sellers ask any questions at all they're invariably the wrong ones. Your questions should be about the role itself and the organisation (below the line) not on what you can get out of the deal (above the line) so remain businesslike and *continue drilling down on their problem* – as soon as you go above the line you stop selling and revert to that person who's just turned up to get a job. Let your competitors do that. *Visualisation* is really important here. At this late stage of the meeting you have done all the hard work and the buyer should already be visualising you in the role. It should be almost as if you are sitting in front of them with that 'hat' on your head. That visualisation is so much stronger if you stay 'below the line' - it weakens if you stray 'above the line'.

Your questions can, and sometimes should be, just as probing as any that they might have asked you. Preparing a few tricky questions is a useful confidence booster. If the buyer is giving you a grilling you can be reassured to know that you have a few 'fast balls' to deliver at the end.

Don't 'overplay' the 'End Game' as you don't want to send the signal that you are just asking questions to impress. Be genuine and stick to the ground rules, which are:

1. Don't interrogate the buyer. Although the meeting is a two-way process there's still that inherent balance of power which by its very nature is weighted on the side of the buyer (who has the cheese) and which it is not in your interests to upset - 'interviewing the interviewer' upsets it.

2. Only ask questions which in your judgment the buyer will be qualified to answer. Doing otherwise can make them feel uncomfortable.

3. Don't ask questions the answers to which you could have reasonably been expected to find out before turning up, e.g. by looking at their website.

4. As we'll see, there are certain questions which are safe to ask at a one to one meeting but which might be inadvisable to put to a larger audience.

5. Although your questions can be just as probing as theirs, and you too can ask supplementary questions, be mindful of your body language (and

theirs). How you frame and deliver your questions can be crucial. Be assertive if necessary but not aggressive–you're still being judged.

6. Have your questions written down and, *providing you feel comfortable with it*, be prepared to refer to what is in effect your agenda. You'll almost certainly be crossing those questions off your list that have been dealt with. Be seen to be doing so. That's giving them tangible evidence to show you're serious about the meeting and have prepared for it.

7. Don't feel it necessary to ask *all* of your questions. Only you can judge when it's time to bring the End Game to a close. Be aware of the time factor and their boredom threshold. Putting tops on pens, the tidying up of paper and furtive glances at the clock are all signs that you're out-staying your welcome.

8. Be prepared to test for consistency. You can ask a question of one buyer at the first meeting and repeat it perhaps some weeks later to one of their colleagues at the second meeting - are they consistent in their responses or does one contradict the other? This can uncover confusion about the role, policy, culture and objectives. If they don't

appear to be singing from the same hymn sheet it might have a bearing on your decision once you've achieved the offer.

9. Prioritise your questions and separate the relevant and necessary from the less relevant and unimportant i.e. distinguish between need to know and nice to know. For example, you might be burning up with curiosity regarding the remuneration and it would be nice to know, but as you don't need to know raising it can, as we've seen, cause problems. For some sellers the hours of work are more important than the salary, perhaps for domestic or travel reasons. But the hours of work can, just like the price, be much more negotiable once you have been awarded the prize, so why ask now?

10. Remember to leave the meeting with your self-respect intact. Although most of the people you meet will not have been trained to interview they will treat you with courtesy and respect - the least we all deserve. But you must always be prepared for the one who may try to intimidate and bully. They are a bad advertisement for their organisation and

you may take the view that if this is how they are treating you now, how will they treat you if you join them? It may be time to deliver that 'fast ball' question.

One seller was being interrogated by her prospective boss, the bullying type - so all was indeed lost, for a quite junior role that had been advertised (as they so often are) as being 'an exciting opportunity'. He brusquely asked if she had any questions and as she knew the game was up she replied with a good 'open' question; "Only one – you advertised this position as being 'an exciting opportunity'. How can you demonstrate this excitement, as I don't feel I have a handle on that?" Predictably he was lost for words and she left the meeting with her head held high. Don't put up with any nonsense or it will become emotional baggage that you will forever carry. They will (or at least should) be drilling down on your CV to test it for credibility. You should, likewise, be prepared to test their sales literature – job advertisements contain a lot of hyperbole (tell me Mr. Buyer, in what sense is your team 'dynamic'?) Very rarely, if ever, will you have to press this 'nuclear button' but always have it in your armoury.

Questions For You To Ask

Or – "Tell me more about your problem." What questions may you legitimately ask? You will, of course, come up with some of your own 'below the line' questions, as you are the expert in your field. But let's add some 'due diligence' questions to your list, and these are the questions that sellers often regret not having asked:

You've done your research about the organisation prior to the meeting, if only to answer their question 'What do you know about us?' But if they don't ask it's frustrating for you to have done that homework but not been given an opportunity to sell it. Insure against this by devising a question of your own which makes the point, e.g. "Your website indicates that... ". Now go on to ask a question about what you picked up from their website.

Why has this vacancy arisen? This may have already been explained or be self evident, but should they be seeking a replacement for the existing incumbent in the role then this may have implications. Their reply may be the enigmatic "The current post-holder is leaving ". Be prepared to probe and ask a supplementary. Avoid the interrogational "why are they leaving?". Frame your question diplomatically; "Are they leaving for any reasons I need to be aware of?" (ungrammatical, but 'gender neutral' and fine when spoken). If there's been a problem with the present incumbent this is inviting them to put it on the table. Observe their body language.

You have a right to know, and a need to know, exactly what happened to any predecessor in the role and the sooner the better. Many a seller has regretted not asking this question – you don't want to turn up on day one and have someone sidle up to you at the water cooler and whisper in your ear "You're in the hot seat now eh – let me tell you what happened to the last one" or "I hope you survive longer than the other three they've had in the last year." If you don't ask now then certainly do so before accepting any offer – accept nothing until you have discovered this or you could be in for an unpleasant surprise in week one. You have to judge when to stop probing but again, read their body language – nanosecond exchanges of glances between buyers might indicate that you're on to something.

They may inform you that the present incumbent is being promoted. That's good news, but you may ask the supplementary question "To what position?" On being told you may choose to ask a further supplementary - "How long were they in the role before being promoted?" This can be a means of testing for consistency. The buyer may have previously done a big selling job on you to encourage you to join them. They may have waxed lyrical about the rapidity of promotion; "We have a policy of not keeping the same person in the same role for more than two years, after that we are looking to move them up in the organisation". This can be highly encouraging early on in the meeting but if during the 'End Game' they admit that the present incumbent has been in post for ten years it's not entirely consistent with their previous statement. If the previous incumbent has left you may be able to track them down on LinkedIn etc and ask their opinion.

If they tell you the present incumbent in the role is being promoted and you show no interest in *their* new position they may interpret this as being *inconsistent* with what you may have said earlier in the meeting (or the previous meeting), or that you are not thinking of sticking around long enough to be promoted.

When is the current post holder leaving? and When are you intending to start the successful applicant?

These are logical supplementary questions you may choose to ask during 'Dead Zone Two', or further down the track as you won't want to appear presumptuous, but armed with the answers you can figure out if there's going to be a 'handover' period. If the two dates don't overlap then there clearly won't be, in which case if you're offered the role while the current post holder is still there it would be wise to suggest that you come in to 'shadow' that person, if only for a day. If they baulk at this sensible suggestion then alarm bells should be ringing. Why don't they want you to meet this person? *Perhaps because they know where the bodies are buried*. Push to get that meeting – in less than two hours that person can tell you things that it could otherwise take you two months to discover, or indeed tell you things that might make your hair stand on end and question the wisdom of accepting the offer.

Did you try to fill the position internally?

A good organisation should try to promote from within before hiring externally, so did they?

A certain response is always worth pursuing: "There was an internal candidate but we felt that he didn't have enough experience". So, an internal candidate has been passed over. It might now be wise to ask how that person reacted to it, because if there is any bridge building to be done you need to know now, not find out by default in three months time that a persistently un-cooperative member of your team wants you to fail because they were passed over for the role.

Never assume that you will be welcomed with open arms by everyone. If this were a 'people management' role then such questions should impress as you are selling your awareness of the importance of getting everyone 'on–side' from day one.

If I were to join your organisation where might you see me in five years time?

Not always appropriate but straight out of the buyers' textbook and as it's a two-way process good enough for the seller. Just asking the question delivers the message that you're thinking of sticking around for at least five years and are looking to progress. Most buyers understand that movement in the market place is frequent and unpredictable, and there's tacit agreement between buyers and sellers that tenure may only be short term, but giving expression to these fundamental truths is still not welcomed in a formal meeting. The expectation remains that sellers should at least send signals of long-term commitment and a desire to progress.

How do you see your organisation developing over the next couple of years?

Providing you judge that the buyer is qualified to venture an opinion this is a safe and useful question.

If nothing else it indicates a degree of interest in their objectives. If the buyer is patently qualified to answer it by virtue of their position e.g. CEO and yet is bereft of ideas, then you just might want to question the wisdom of joining a company that doesn't know where it's heading.

Exercise caution about asking this question of a panel. One of the dilemmas with panels is that as an outsider you wouldn't know the political backcloth or the personal friendships/enmities. You could be lighting the blue touch paper and not know it. Alienating a panel member is easily done with an injudicious question in front of his/her peers. A possible sign that you've broken ground rule 4 is when you provoke the 'pass the parcel' response as in (turning to another member of the panel) "You might want to field that question John?"

What would you see as my main priority in this role? Is there anything you think one should get to grips with sooner rather than later?

During these meetings buyers do not always make a good job of describing the work that needs to be done, and it's not unusual to reach the concluding stages and still feel that you haven't got a precise enough understanding of it. This is a way of teasing it out without coming across as a complete ignoramus. It can also encourage the buyer to reveal for the first time a fundamental if not serious problem, which they had hitherto not mentioned. In such ways can you discover if you are being invited to drink from a poisoned chalice.

This can be a useful question to test for consistency; ask it of someone else at the next meeting and you may find that they come up with a different response. Others may be of the opinion that the work needing to be done is unnecessary. Events are changing so quickly in the competitive, particularly hi-tech, market place that a slow moving recruitment process can't always keep up. From initial advertisement to final appointment can take three months or more. Events can have changed so much in that time frame that the role has either fundamentally changed or no longer exists.

May I take a look around before leaving?

For valid reasons the answer may well be 'No'. They haven't built this into the schedule, they've no one available to take you around or they simply hadn't thought of it. No matter - showing an interest in the working environment will send positive signals. If the meeting has gone well the question will often elicit a positive response indicating that you have got through to the next stage; "Not today, but we'll show you around next time." This question can be vital for certain types of organisation. What are they in business to sell or provide - a service or a product? If, for example, you are talking to a manufacturer, and if they make the product on the site of your meeting, never leave that meeting without asking if you can see the production process. Many a seller has blown it by showing no interest in the product. Waiting for the invitation to look around is no good at all - buyers will often put the onus on you to ask. In particular, if you are in the early stage of your career and wish to progress do ask questions *outside the remit* and *beyond the scope* of the role you are discussing; show an interest in the business as a whole as that sets you apart and demonstrates that you have potential. Yes, you are still 'painting the picture' and 'adding colour' during the End Game.

Regardless of the type of business, never accept an offer without having seen where you will be working. A sub-standard working environment can have a strong influence on your decision, and the working environment can be very different from that in which the meetings took place. Don't be seduced by that 'corporate plumage' - it's there for the customers and clients, not you. It really is surprising how many sellers accept an offer without seeing where they would be working. We spend more time at work these days than we spend at home. You wouldn't buy a house without looking around.

I've enjoyed our discussion. I'm confident I can take this on and do it really well, but do you have any reservations about my suitability for it?

If you choose to ask this it will be your penultimate question. You may ask it at a first or subsequent meeting. You should certainly be inclined to ask it at a one to one meeting which you feel has gone well and at which there has been good rapport with the buyer. If it's clear to you that the meeting has been a complete dog's breakfast then perhaps best not to ask – as you may detect the thought bubble: "Reservations! That's like looking for hay in a haystack. How much time do you have?" Judge it right and it's a 'no lose' question for you. They either have a reservation or they don't so why not find out where the buyer stands on this? Should there be no reservations you're inviting them to say so. Psychologically this makes it more difficult, though not impossible, for them to subsequently send you a rejection.

You're really saying to the buyer; 'I want to get hired and I've told you why you should do so - do you see any reasons why you shouldn't hire me?' If the buyer responds by saying, in effect, 'No - I don't have a reason why I shouldn't hire you.' then the outcome has got to be 'Well, hire me then'. Now of course that dialogue isn't actually taking place but that is the undertow.

Moreover, should all your instincts be telling you that this is truly the right problem for you to solve never be fearful of *telling the buyer that you want it*.

Few sellers are confident enough to be this direct but if expressed in the right manner and at the right time it can have a profound psychological effect. In a buyers' market they have an embarrassment of riches and if it's a tight decision between yourself and a competitor it's most likely to be offered to the one who *said* they wanted it - and yes, the margin between winning and losing can be that slim. Of course, events may subsequently unfold that may impel you to decline the role but no matter - your objective is to *get the offer*.

When the buyer doesn't have a reservation the best answer you could normally expect is (after a short silence) " We can't make a decision today (you haven't asked for a decision – only a businesslike opinion) as we've others to interview but no, I've enjoyed our discussion too (they mirror this back to you) and I have no reservations but we'll have to see how the other candidates compare". I have known buyers respond to this by saying - " I have no reservations at all – when can you start?" **[+]**

But what if the buyer *does* have a reservation? Well, this could be your last chance to defend against it so it's only in your interests to encourage them to put it on the table. If you don't they'll still have it when you've made your exit and you can't do anything about it then. So in this instance the penultimate question can be your 'get out of jail' card. We have already seen that these meetings are all about selling yourself to get hired and defending yourself against objections to hiring you. *You can only deal with an objection if it's voiced.*

Uncovering the hidden objections is a key part of your strategy and buyers are more disposed to do this at the end rather than at the beginning of a meeting. At the end a certain rapport should have been built up which may not have existed at the start. Once a climate of mutual respect has been established the buyer will feel more comfortable in voicing a sensitive issue - most hidden objections revolve around sensitive issues.

Although there may not be much time left for you to defend yourself against an objection raised at this late stage you'll be able to take it away with you, give it more thought and put up a more considered defence in your follow up e-mail (page 229).

Should you ask this question of a panel? Perhaps not as they haven't had the opportunity to confer and you are less likely to elicit a meaningful response. However, on some occasions you will know, perhaps through a network contact on the inside, that they share a strong reservation. If they haven't raised it you may as well put the question on the table. The preamble to your question is important. Never ask it simply by saying 'Do you have any reservations about my suitability for it?' as that is weak and it implies that *you* might have some. Starting your preamble by saying 'I've enjoyed our discussion....' encourages the buyer to begin their response in the same vein. And in saying "I'm confident I can take this on and do it really well" you are making your position clear.

This penultimate question also gives buyers the opportunity, for which they may be grateful, to return to an issue discussed earlier but on which you failed to convince them. For example " I know we covered this earlier, but I'm still concerned about ......" This is their way of saying 'I'm not convinced but maybe just one more piece of evidence from you will swing it.' With any luck, in the intervening period your brain has been working overtime and now a piece of defensive ammunition you omitted to fire earlier may occur to you. Try not to leave buyers with an objection that will fester after you have left the meeting.

When will I hear from you?

Before you exit, encourage the buyer to make a firm commitment about what happens next and when. Failure to do so may lead to loss of control and should you need to regain the initiative by following up it's helpful for you to have established when it would be legitimate to do so.

Subsequently taking the view that 'no news is good news' is mere self-delusion and there's no virtue in not knowing. Should they fail to meet their own deadline then you may want to chase them up. The outcome of the meeting will always be at the top of your priority list but rarely will it be at the top of theirs – for the buyer this recruitment process is a side-show, not the main event - they have a business to run. Don't allow yourself to be fobbed off with 'we'll be in touch as soon as possible'. Pin them down by giving two options "Friday? Or maybe next Friday?" Try to make them commit. Once they've made a commitment then you'll know it's legitimate to chase them if you haven't heard by the due date. If it does happen to be a Friday then don't delay that call until Friday afternoon, otherwise someone will inform you that 'She's gone away for the week-end'. 11 a.m. Friday should do it.

Looking at your campaign in the round there may of course be times when you *won't* want to follow up, and may be desperate for them *not* to get that answer to you by Friday. For example this role may not be your first choice. It may be your first choice role on which you are following up, or indeed not following up; sometimes silence from you really can speak a thousand words (page 62) and swing the balance of power (page 132) in your favour.

----------♦ ♦ ♦----------

Dead Zone Two And The 'Columbo Question'

Once the meeting has been formally concluded you'll enter a new phase, of unpredictable length and indeterminate nature, before you leave the premises. For dramatic effect let's call this 'Dead Zone Two', and it can kick in sooner than you might think. For example, at the conclusion of a final meeting the buyer (in all probability your potential boss) is waxing lyrical about your joining the business and makes what appears to be a spontaneous decision. Reaching for the phone the buyer says, "Hey, if Joe Soap is free I'll take you up to see him to talk about terms and conditions" (which haven't been previously discussed). Having established by phone that, as luck would have it, Joe is indeed free the buyer says: "let's go" and steers you out of the office. You are now in Dead Zone Two, from which you want to emerge in one piece, so tread carefully. This Zone is fertile ground for much 'small talk' and you may feel your 'social hat' (Building Block 4) settling comfortably on your head. Typically, it's taken a while to reach Joe's office so you find yourself being ushered into a comfortable chair in some 'reception' area "while I just make sure Joe is still free." You're now snoozing and basking in your success - you think the interaction is over. Awoken from your reverie you find that the buyer, having turned smartly on his heel, is now looming over you and, feigning forgetfulness, hits you with the 'Columbo question': "Oh, just one more thing - what salary are you looking for?" Our delaying tactics and lengthy sound bites don't work in the Dead Zone. A 'social hat' looks up like a startled rabbit and plucks a figure out of the air, whereupon the buyer turns smartly on his heel to tell Joe the opening price. A 'business hat' will deliver a passable 'beats me' impression and profess to have 'an open mind', thus sending the buyer away empty handed. The 'Columbo Question' doesn't have to be about the price but it invariably is.

An accomplished 'Dead Zone' operator will ask pointed 'small talk' questions which are really 'Why shouldn't I hire you?' questions with the tie loosened such as 'Are you talking to other organisations?', dressed up here as 'How's the job search going?' (It's always going well) or the more enigmatic 'If you could choose any job what would it be?'.

But the Dead Zone is also a two way process so you too can ask 'Columbo' questions in a more informal manner, which may not have seemed appropriate during the more formal 'End Game'. For example, 'How many other people are you seeing?' and 'When are you looking to start the successful applicant?' The answers to these give an indication as to what you're up against in terms of competition and time, and consequently what leverage you may have to negotiate on the price at a later date. You can also seize the moment to ask 'Do you have a business card?' Thus ensuring that you leave with an e-mail address to send your 'thanks for your time' message. You may also show an interest in the buyer on a more personal level; 'Have you worked here for long?' And even 'Do you enjoy it?' Closed questions but fit for purpose in the Dead Zone.

---------♦ ♦ ♦---------

Who's Got The Ball?

We saw earlier how it can be useful to see the communication between buyer and seller in terms of a 'tennis match'. After the meeting has concluded it's helpful to revisit this. You might think that the buyer 'has the ball', i.e. judgments have been made about you and conclusions will have been drawn - all you can now do is sit back and await the result. In reality you have the ball, and communication from you at this stage can have immense impact.

'Thank you' letters get people hired and as there's no time to be lost e-mail is more appropriate in this situation. Firstly, and immediately after the meeting because it's fresh in your mind, make notes about what took place. You may not be attending a further meeting with them for some weeks and you'll need some notes to which you can refer prior to that next meeting, and if you are having many meetings discussing different problems you can totally confuse yourself between what you sold at one meeting and what you sold at another.

Make your own assessment. Perhaps there were aspects that with hindsight you could have handled better. Perhaps in answer to your 'penultimate question' they raised an objection that you had little time to deal with, or you omitted to mention a crucial fact that might have reassured them. It's not too late. The 'thank you' message, apart from being courteous, can get you a second meeting that you may not have secured - it exploits (in the best sense of the word) that window of time between when they have made a decision *but before they have conveyed it to you.* After the meeting it doesn't usually take buyers long to make a decision but it can take them an inordinate length of time to convey it, because this is, for them, a sideshow, but what are their options?

1. Your overall performance was so poor that they never want to meet you again under any circumstances. A 'thank you' message from you won't reverse that decision.

2. You blew them away and have already been placed on the short list of say, three people, in which

case a 'thank you' message will reinforce that positive decision and steal a march on the other two.

3. You performed well; they liked you and might well have decided to see you again. However, it's a buyers' market and the short list of three has already been mentally drawn up and you're not on it. This is like a golfer not quite making 'the cut' to play in the next round – the margins are slim. So with mixed feelings and much regret they'll eventually get around to sending you a rejection or, if a recruitment firm is involved, get them to give you the message. Your communication can prevent this from happening and get you to that final meeting. It's unlikely that even those in 2 above will have taken the initiative to communicate. That you have bothered to do so can have a powerful effect.

'Further to our meeting (note: 'meeting' not 'interview') *this morning I would like to confirm my interest in the position. I enjoyed our discussion and please pass my thanks on to* (if you met a colleague). *Thanks also for your hospitality* (if they gave you any) *and for taking the time to show me around* (if they did so).

Incidentally, you may recall we briefly discussed (whatever it was) *I omitted to mention that...* (briefly – don't make a big deal of it). *This additional information may be helpful to you in reaching your decision.'*

Now we know it's a decision they've probably already made (but not conveyed) but which of the above categories are you in? If you feel that there are no objections to be overcome then don't invent one. The importance here is that you are bothering to say 'thank you for your time' and confirming your ongoing interest in their problem.

'Job beggars' (in all likelihood your competitors) are most reluctant to assert themselves in this way following their 'interview' as they feel it in some way 'breaks the rules'. In truth, they don't consider doing it at all. And yet they are often the very people who, had they been in work and come away from a business meeting with a customer, wouldn't think twice about sending a follow up e-mail to say 'thanks' or clarify a point.

It must be said that there are also some buyers, and these are the one's who still believe they are 'interviewing you' for a 'job', who take the view 'If you didn't tell me at the interview it's too late now.' This is of course a ludicrous stance to take. To make the right decision they need all the facts they can get, and if you didn't give them all the facts then the sensible ones would rather have the missing information after the meeting than not at all.

---------♦ ♦ ♦---------

Extending The Olive Branch

With positive thinking you can still get an offer and win the prize even when you've lost it, but only if you communicate.

The cruellest blow is when you've had a number of meetings with the buyer, jumped through all the hoops but fallen at the final hurdle. It's highly probable that if you got to the short list you could have solved their problem. A short list will typically comprise three 'winners', i.e. perfectly acceptable sellers. If buyers could hire all three they probably would, but with only one problem to solve two rejections have to be sent, reluctantly.

From the buyers' perspective, and from bitter experience, what can go wrong will go wrong. As we now know, they are often no more experienced in the art of buying than you feel you are at selling. They may presume, for example, that the chosen one will bite their hand off at the first sniff of an offer and they will be precipitate in sending out the rejection letters. The winner may, many days later, proceed to negotiate on the remuneration and the relationship may founder. The winner (perhaps the one with all the experience) may go as far as starting, and even be two or three months into, the role only to leave at short notice because it isn't stretching them and they've received a better offer. Either party can discover that they have made the wrong decision. In short, the blind date went well but there's typically a three-month 'courtship' period between buyer and seller during which a falling out can take place. You can capitalise on this. Buyers can feel uncomfortable about going back 'cap in hand' to sellers they've rejected, for they'll always know they were second choice. Make it easier for them to come back to you, not the other seller they rejected, by extending the olive branch and knocking the following ball back over the net:

'I am naturally disappointed to have been unsuccessful on this occasion (you haven't given up – still selling tenacity). However, I would like to thank you for your courtesy in seeing me, I really enjoyed our discussions and as I retain my strong interest in working with your organisation do not hesitate to come back to me (implication-not the other winner) should the situation change (if it all ends in tears) in the near future.'

Because your emotions may be running high after getting their rejection the above message is not one that you will much feel like sending, and resist the natural inclination to inject an element of 'sour grapes' into it as that questions their judgment. But if you send it don't be surprised to get a call, maybe some days, weeks or even months later, asking if you're still available.

Again, exercise your judgment on this but consider sending this communication as a letter because this isn't time critical and a letter is more classy, tangible and memorable.

Dealing positively with rejection is one of the keys to success. Job beggars take it personally. So personally that some will refuse to re-open a dialogue, at any subsequent time in their career, with a buyer that declined to buy what they were selling the first time around. That would be a crazy way to run a business.

Conclusion

There's no lack of guidance on 'how to be interviewed' and no shortage of people all too willing to give you wise counsel on 'interview technique'. Yet this guidance is invariably based on the premise that all 'interviewers' have been trained in the art of 'interviewing' – that they know what they are looking for and how to find it. In my experience, and that of the thousands of 'sellers' and 'buyers' I have worked with, this is rarely the case.

They also approach the subject from the standpoint of 'interviewee' as 'job beggar', which perpetuates the 'sit up straight, give a firm handshake and maintain eye contact' mind-set which is both patronising and less than helpful.

There's little point in preparing 'interviewees' for the 'jobs market' as we would like it to be or as it perhaps was in the 20th Century. That was a time when we were taught to believe that employers were doing us a favour in hiring us; that they should be treated with reverence and that they were somehow, well, a different species. That's never been the case and career coaches soon discover that when buyers lose *their* jobs they have the same fears, make the same mistakes, and are just as incapable at selling themselves as the rest of us, simply because they are human, just like you and me. So, when you get hired (and you will get hired) you may become a buyer and have to recruit someone someday. Remember how it was.

The 21st Century market place is already an infinitely more fast moving, vibrant, changing, unpredictable and competitive market and one where even the boundaries between who is selling and who is buying are becoming blurred. To survive as individuals we must all have something to sell that others want to buy. We must learn to diversify and build our portfolios. We must accustom ourselves to becoming itinerant workers, but perhaps above all we must discover the art of persuading others to buy what we have to sell. 'Winning At Interview' has prepared you for the market place as it is and as it is likely to be in the foreseeable future.

Alan Jones helps people to find the right job. He is the author of several books on job search and career building including 'How To Negotiate Your Salary' and 'Network To Get Work.'

Index of Questions

42 Questions - The Answer To Everything

How was your journey?	79
Tell me about yourself	80
Your CV - it's all hype isn't it?	90
What do you know about us?	92
Why does this job interest you?	94
Why are you leaving?	95
Why did you stay with them so long?	102
You've done a lot of job-hopping - why?	105
What is your greatest strength?	106
What is your greatest weakness?	110
Where do you see yourself in five years?	123
What is your greatest achievement?	125
What was your biggest mistake?	127
What problems were there in your last role?	129
Are you having discussions with other organisations?	131

Who are you speaking with?	135
How does this role compare?	136
Are you ambitious?	137
If you were recruiting for this role what qualities would you be seeking?	139
Do you have an aggressive management style?	141
Do you prefer working on your own or in a team?	146
If you could choose any job what would it be?	147
Who was your last boss?	148
If I asked your last boss about you what do you think he/she would tell me?	149
What was his/her greatest weakness?	151
Has your career developed as you would have liked?	153
Would you be prepared to relocate?	156
Have you ever failed in any job you have tried to do?	158

If one of your team ceased to perform what would you do about it?	163
How do you motivate people?	164
Would you accept this position if we offered it to you?	165
Why haven't you found a job yet?	169
How important is money to you?	171
You do not have all the experience we are seeking.	175
Don't you think you are over-qualified/too experienced?	184
What can you offer us?	186
What would you expect to achieve in your first 100 days?	187
Do you ever have doubts about your ability to do a job?	188
If the interests of your boss and your staff conflicted, with whom would you side?	189

What was your previous salary?	191
What salary are you seeking?	196

Printed in Great Britain
by Amazon